Kathleen O´Meara

The bells of the sanctuary : Mary Benedicta, Agnes, Aline, one of God's heroines, Monseigneur Darboy

Kathleen O'Meara

The bells of the sanctuary : Mary Benedicta, Agnes, Aline, one of God's heroines, Monseigneur Darboy

ISBN/EAN: 9783337305260

Hergestellt in Europa, USA, Kanada, Australien, Japan

Cover: Foto ©Lupo / pixelio.de

Weitere Bücher finden Sie auf **www.hansebooks.com**

The Bells of the Sanctuary:

MARY BENEDICTA,

AGNES, ALINE, ONE OF GOD'S HEROINES,

MONSEIGNEUR DARBOY.

BY

KATHLEEN O'MEARA
(GRACE RAMSAY),
AUTHOR OF 'IZA'S STORY,' 'THOMAS GRANT,' 'FREDERIC OZANAM,' ETC.

LONDON: BURNS AND OATES.
1879.
[*Right of Translation reserved.*]

CONTENTS.

	PAGE
MARY BENEDICTA	3
AGNES	63
ALINE	119
ONE OF GOD'S HEROINES	191
MONSEIGNEUR DARBOY	257

MARY BENEDICTA.

MARY BENEDICTA.

WE little dreamed, either of us, in those mischief-loving days of frolic and fun, that she was one day to be a saint, and that I should tell her story.

Yet, look well at the face. Is there not something like a promise of sainthood on the pure white brow? And the eyes, blue-grey Irish eyes, with the dark lashes throwing a shadow underneath—'diamonds put in with dirty fingers'—do they not speak to you with a promise, a revelation of some 'open vision,' whose coming dawn already reflects a beauty within, far beyond what meets your gaze? Yet though it seems so clear now in the retrospect, this prophetic side of her beauty, I own that it never struck me then. I am going to tell her story simply, with strict accuracy as regards the traits of her character, of her life and her death; and I shall tell the bad with the good, neither seeking to varnish her faults, nor to heighten by any dramatic colouring the beautiful reality of her virtues. The history is one calculated, it seems to me, to be a light and a lesson to many; the very faults and follies, the strange beginning so unlike the end, all taken as parts of a whole in the true experience of a soul, have a teaching in them whose truth and simplicity is its best and truest eloquence.

Her early career was the wildest that ever convent school-girl lived through. High-spirited, reckless, utterly defiant of rules, wild as an antelope, she was the torment of her teachers and the delight of her companions. Her good nature and good temper carried her serenely above all the petty jealousies and wranglings that mark that little miniature world, a School; and her spirit of turbulent independence, whilst it was constantly getting her into scrapes, was so redeemed by an abhorrence of everything approaching to deceit or meanness, that it did not prevent her being a universal favourite with the Nuns. One in particular, a rigid disciplinarian, who was the terror of the school, and in a state of permanent war with Mary (this was her real Christian name), was even less proof than the others against the indomitable sweetness and lovableness of her rebellious pupil, and occasionally, after a hot skirmish carried on before the public, viz. the second class, Mother Benedicta would take the rebel aside, and actually try to coax her into an apology, or a promise of conversion. Sometimes she succeeded, for the refractory young lady was always more amenable to gentleness than to stern reason, and was besides, in spite of the war-footing on which they stood, fondly attached to Mother Benedicta; but she never pledged herself unconditionally. This was a great grievance with Mother Benedicta. She used to argue and plead and scold by the hour, in order to induce Mary to give 'her word of honour' that she would observe such and such a prohibition, or obey such and such a rule—silence was generally the *casus belli*—but all to no purpose.

'No, Sister, I promise you to try; but I won't promise to do, or not to do,' she would answer undefiantly, but quite resolutely.

'If she gave her word of honour to be a saint, I do believe she would be one,' Mother Benedicta was sometimes heard to say, with a sigh, after one of those long conferences which ended, as usual, in the conditional 'I'll try, Sister.' 'If I could but get Mary to promise me outright to mend her ways, I need never take any more trouble about her.'

I mention this little incident advisedly, for

though at the time her pupils thought, in their wisdom, that it must be pure perversity on the part of the Mistress that made her so pursue Mary on the subject, seeing that they were, most of them, in the habit of pledging their 'word of honour' any given number of times a week without any particular result, many of them lived to see that, in dealing with this individual character, Mother Benedicta was guided by prophetic instinct.

She never succeeded, however, during the four years that Mary was under her charge. This sort of drawn battle in which they were engaged to the last, did not prevent, nevertheless, a tender and strong affection from existing between the two belligerents. It was a habit with the girls to adopt the name of their favourite Nun and add it to their own ; Mary followed this custom, and even after she left school continued to sign herself 'Mary Benedicta.'

When the time came round for frequenting the Sacraments, it was the sure signal for a row between the mistress and pupil. There was no plea or stratagem to which Mary would not have recourse in order to shirk going to confession. She had nevertheless a kind of reputation for piety amongst her companions, a queer impulsive sort of piety peculiar to herself; they believed to a great extent in her prayers, and when they were in any evil plight she was one of those they habitually appealed to to pray for them; not perhaps with any precise view as to the spiritual quality of the prayers, but impressed by her general character that, whatever she did, she did thoroughly, and was sure to put her whole heart in.

The one point that Mother Benedicta clung to as a sheet anchor in Mary's spiritual condition was her devotion to the Blessed Sacrament. But this displayed itself solely, as far as outward observers could see, in an enthusiastic love for Benediction; and as Mary was passionately fond of music, and confessed to a weakness for effective ceremonials, Mother Benedicta had occasional misgivings as to how much of the devotion really went to the object of the ceremony and how much to its accessories: the organ, the lights, and the incense. As to the rules of the school, she systematically ignored them. The Rule of Silence she looked upon as below contempt—a device fit for fools, but unworthy the observance of rational beings. To the last day of her sojourn in the Convent she practically illustrated the opinion that speech was of gold and silence of brass, and she left it with the reputation of being the greatest talker, and the most untidy and unruly subject, but the sweetest nature that had ever tried the patience and won the hearts of the Community.

She spent a year at home, and then her father placed her at the Sacré Cœur in Paris. She was now eighteen, and her education at this advanced period was in a sadly retrograde state. Masters had been lavished on her without any regard to expense while she was at school in Ireland, but the little she had learnt had been assiduously forgotten in the course of a year's wild holiday at home, when all kind of reading, and even her favourite music, were left aside for the more congenial pastimes of dancing, and skating, and flying across country after the hounds.

My mother was living in Paris, and Mary was placed under her wing. We went to see her on the *jours de parloir*, and she came to us on the *jours de sortie*. But, as might have been expected, the sudden change from a life of perfect freedom and constant out-door exercise to one of complete seclusion and sedentary habits, proved too trying to her health. After three months the medical man of the Convent declared that he was not prepared to accept the responsibility of taking charge of her, and strongly recommended her being sent home. We communicated this intelligence to her father, begging at the same time that, before he came to remove her, she might be allowed to spend a month with us. The request was granted, and Mary came to stay with us.

That we might lose as little as possible of each other's company while we were together, she shared my room. We spent the morning at home, I studying — I was continuing my education with masters—she reading or lolling about the room while I took my lessons, watching the clock, and longing for the hour to come that would set me free and let us go out.

My mother, who only in a lesser degree shared my affection for the beautiful undisciplined girl, was anxious to make her visit as pleasant as possible, and took her about to all the places best worth seeing—the galleries, the palaces, the museums, the churches. The latter, though many of them, even as works of art, were among the most interesting monuments for a stranger's inspection, Mary seemed provokingly indifferent to, and when we entered one, instead of kneeling a moment before the Sanctuary as a Catholic does from natural impulse and force of habit, she would just make the necessary genuflexion, and, without waiting for us, walk on round the building alone, as if impelled by irresistible curiosity at once to examine the pictures or the stained glass, and then make her exit with as little delay as might be. This strange shrinking from the churches did not strike my mother, who was apt to remain all the time at her prayers, while I went round doing the honours of the place to Mary; but it struck me, and it pained and puzzled me. She was too innately honest to attempt the shadow of prevarication even in her attitude, and her haste in 'doing' every church we entered was so undisguised that she evidently did not care whether I noticed it or not. Once on coming out of the little Church of Sainte Geneviève—one of the loveliest shrines ever raised to the worship of God by the genius of man—I said rather sharply to her, for she had beaten a more precipitate retreat than usual, and cut short my mother's devotions at the tomb of the Saint:

'Mary, one really would think that the devil was at your heels the moment you enter a church, you are always in such a violent hurry to get out of it.'

She laughed. Not mockingly; with a sort of half-ashamed expression, and turning her pure full eyes on me:

'I hate to stay anywhere under false appearances,' she said, still smiling, though there was something grave almost to sadness in the look and voice with which she said it; 'and I always feel such a hypocrite kneeling before the Blessed Sacrament! When I have been there over five minutes, I feel as if I were going to choke.'

I felt shocked, and I suppose I looked it.

'Don't look at me as if I were possessed of the devil!' she said, laughing, but looking confused; 'I mean to be converted by and by; but, *en attendant*, let me have my fling, and, above all, don't preach to me!'

'I hadn't the least intention,' I replied.

'You think I'm gone beyond it, I suppose,' she said. 'Well, you can pray for me; I'm not gone beyond that at any rate.'

This was the only serious conversation, if it deserves the name, that we had during the first week that she was with us.

She enjoyed her visit thoroughly, throwing the zest of her earnest nature into everything—the people and their 'odd French ways,' as she called them, the shops and their exquisite wares, the opera, the gay Bois, with the brilliant throng of fashion that passed round and round the lake every day at the hour of the promenade; the novelty of the scene and the place altogether enchanted her, and there was something quite exhilarating in witnessing the delight she took in it all.

One evening, after a long day of sight-seeing, we were invited by a friend of hers to dine at the *table d'hôte* of the Louvre. It was the *grande nouveauté* just then, and Mary was, consequently, wild to see it. We went. During dinner the admiration excited by her beauty was so glaringly expressed by the persistent stare of every eye within range of her at the table, that my mother was seriously annoyed at having brought her there and exposed her to such an ordeal. But Mary was as blissfully unconscious of the effect she was producing as she was of the cause. I am keeping strictly to the truth in saying that she was perfectly unconscious of her own beauty as far as having any internal perception of it, or complacency in it. This unconcern, which extended to her whole personal appearance, pervaded her habits, and made her sadly careless about her dress. She retained her old fault of untidiness, which had been such a cause of contention with Mother Benedicta, and it was all I could do to get her to put on her clothes straight, and tie her bonnet-strings under her chin and not under her ear when she came out with us.

But to return to the Louvre. We had arranged that when dinner was over we would walk across to the Palais Royal and let Mary see the diamond shops, and all the other wonderful shops, illuminated; but during dessert she overhead some one say that the Emperor was expected that evening at the Grand Opera, and her first impulse of course was to take a box and go there. Her friend at once acceded. My mother, however, objected. I quite forget on what grounds, but they were strong enough at any rate to overrule the plan. With evident disappointment, but, as usual, with the sweetest good humour, Mary gave way. It was then proposed that, before going to the Palais Royal, we should walk on to the Rue Lepeletier and see the Emperor and Empress alight. There was no difficulty in the way of this amendment, so it was adopted. But on coming out of the Louvre we found, to our surprise and discomfiture, that the weather had been plotting against our little programme. The ground, which was frozen dry and hard when we drove down the Champs Elysées little more than an hour before, had become as slippery as glass under a heavy fall of sleet; the horses were already beginning to slip about in a very uncomfortable way, and there was a manifest disinclination on the part of pedestrians to trust themselves into cabs. Apparently it was decreed that Mary was not to see the Emperor and Empress on any terms that night, for it would have been absurdly imprudent to venture on the macadam of the Boulevards, and increase the risk of driving at all by waiting till the streets were so slippery that no horse could keep his footing on them. There was nothing for it but to drive straight home, which we did, going at a foot-pace all the way. It was a memorable night, this one of which I am chronicling a trivial recollection; trivial in itself, but not in its consequences, either negative or positive. It was the 14th of January 1858. We went to bed, and slept, no doubt, soundly. None the less soundly for the thundering crash, which, before we lay down, had shaken the Rue Lepeletier, and the streets and the Boulevard adjoining it, and put out the gas and shattered to powder every window in the vicinity of the Opera. The noise shook half Paris awake that long night. The Boulevards were swarming with the population, indignant and terrified. In the pitch darkness that followed instantaneously on the bursting of the bombs, it was impossible to know, even approximately, how many were murdered or how many were wounded. As was generally the case, a considerable number of strangers had come to see their majesties alight, and both sides of the street were lined with crowds of people. The confusion, therefore, that ensued on the explosion was beyond all description. The number of the victims was immensely exaggerated, and the night resounded with the shrieks and lamentations of women, the plunging and moaning of horses, dying or wounded, and cries of ' *Vive l'Empereur!*' intermingled with men's curses on the fiends who, to secure the murder of one, had sacrificed the lives of hundreds. While this ghastly tumult was scaring away sleep and silence from the city, close at hand, we slept on, all unconscious of what we had escaped. It was only next morning, on going out early, that the *concierge* stopped my mother to tell her the news of the attempt on the Emperor's life.

And we had been vexed and impatient at the rain that drove us home and prevented our going to stand amongst the sight-seers in the Rue Lepeletier!

I shall never forget Mary's face when we told her at breakfast what had happened on the very spot where she had been so bent on going.

Although Orsini's attempt comes merely as an event into my narrative, I cannot resist making a momentary digression in that direction. My readers will, no doubt, remember the extraordinary stoicism displayed by the Emperor at the moment of the explosion. The horses were killed under his carriage, which was violently shaken by the plunging of the terrified animals, and a splinter from one of the shells, flashing through the window, grazed him on the temple. In the midst of the universal panic of the scene one of the equerries rushed forward, flung open the door of the carriage, and taking the Emperor by the arm, cried hurriedly :

'Descendez, sire, descendez !'

'Baissez le marche-pied !' replied his master, and quietly waited till it was done before he moved. He entered the House amidst deafening cheers, and sat out the representation as coolly, and, to all appearance, with as much attention, as if nothing had occurred to ruffle him, now and then merely drawing his handkerchief across the splinter-mark on his forehead, from which the blood oozed slightly.

Next day a solemn Mass of thanksgiving was celebrated in the chapel of the Tuileries. The Empress wished the little prince, then a baby in arms, to be present at the Te Deum for his father's and her almost miraculous preservation. The Court and the Diplomatic body were assembled in the Salle des Maréchaux when the child was carried in by his nurse. He immediately stretched out his hands to his father, clamouring to go to him. The Emperor took him in his arms, and the child, looking up into his face, noticed the ugly red scratch on the temple.

'Papa, *bobo?*'* he lisped, and put up his little hand to touch it.

The hard sphinx-like face struggled for a moment, but the child's touch had melted the strong man's pride; he clasped him to his heart, and literally shook with sobs.

This incident, which was probably never written before, was told to me by an eye-witness on her return from assisting at the Te Deum in the Tuileries.

That night when Mary and I were alone, we talked over the diabolical act which, within four-and-twenty hours, had shaken the whole country like an earthquake, and over the merciful interposition that had checked us on our way to what might have been an awful and instantaneous death. She

* A French baby's expression for *hurt*.

seemed deeply impressed, and though she said little, what she did say disclosed a depth and strength of religious emotion which revealed her to me in quite a new light. It was agreed that she was to go to Confession next day, and we were to say a Novena together in thanksgiving for our preservation.

'Mary,' I said suddenly, after we had been silent for a while, 'why have you such a dislike to approach the Sacraments? I cannot understand how, believing in them at all, you can be satisfied to receive them so seldom.'

'It is not dislike,' she replied; 'it's precisely because I believe in them so intensely, because I realise so awfully the power and sanctity of the Eucharist, that I keep away. I shrink from committing myself. If I went often to Holy Communion, I should have to detach myself from everything, and to give up my whole life to preparing for it. I know I should, and I don't want to do it —not yet, at any rate,' she added absently, as if speaking to herself.

I shall never forget the effect the words had upon me, nor her face as she uttered them. The night was far spent; the emotions of the day, the long watch, and perhaps the flickering light of our candle that was burning low, all conspired to give an unusual pallor to her features, which imbued them with an almost ethereal delicacy. I always think of her now, as she sat there in her girlish white drapery, her hands locked together on her knees, her head thrown back, and her eyes looking up, so still and rapt, as if some distant horizon were breaking on her gaze and transfixing it. Nothing broke on mine. In my dull blindness I did not see that I was assisting at the birth of a great mystery, a spectacle on which the gaze of angels was riveted; the wrestling of a soul with God, the soul resisting, the Creator pleading and pursuing.

She left us at the end of January to return home. We parted with many tears, and promises to correspond often, and think of each other constantly. For a time we did correspond very regularly. For nearly a year. During this period her life was an unpausing whirl of gaieties. Balls, visits, concerts, operas followed each other during the season, to be succeeded in the country by more balls and visits, hunting parties, and the usual round of amusements that make up gay country life. Mary was everywhere the acknowledged beauty of the place, the admired of all admirers.

Strange to say, in spite of her 'success,' she made no enemies. Though, indeed, it would have been perhaps stranger if she had. Her sweet artless manner, and perfect unconsciousness of self, went for at least as much as her beauty in the admiration she excited. If she danced every dance at every ball it was never once for the pleasure of saying she did it, of triumphing over any other girl, but for the pure delight of dancing. If others saw her followed by a train of beseeching partners, while they were left 'making tapestry,' as the French say, it was so clearly none of her own seeking, as far as mere coquetry went, that however they might envy her, they could not be angry with her. I am not trying to make folly look like wisdom, or to justify the levity of the life Mary was leading at this time; I am only anxious to convey a true idea of the spirit in which she lived it: reckless exuberance of spirits, the zest of youth in the gay opportunities that showered upon her path. The spirit of worldliness in its true and worst sense did not possess her; it did not even touch her; its corroding breath had not withered her soul, or hardened her heart; both were uncorrupted. She was waltzing through flames without suspecting any danger, like a child letting off rockets, and clapping hands at the pretty blue blaze, while no thought of peril interferes to mar its innocent enjoyment of the feat.

I set this down that it may not seem as if Mary were playing a deliberate game with God ; bidding Him wait till she was ready for Him ; till she was tired of the world, and the world of her, and had drunk her fill of its delights. No ; she was utterly incapable of such a base and guilty calculation. She had simply forgotten all about her soul. Those mysterious pleadings which had formerly—especially on that night of the 15th of January—stirred its fibres and called out transient yearnings after the higher life, had ceased to visit her. She was intoxicated with the sense of youth and happiness, and had flung herself into the dance of life till her head reeled. But all the stir and foam were on the surface ; the depths below were sleeping.

One thing which never abandoned her in her most dissipated days was a tender love for the poor. She used to say herself that this was the finger by which she had held on to God without knowing it. Many are the touching traits told of her charity by the suffering and the destitute round her father's home. Once, on a bitter winter's day, she came upon an old woman crouched under a hedge, trying to shelter herself from the cold ; she did not ask for an alms, but Mary was so moved by the sight of her rags that she immediately slipped off her own flannel petticoat and wrapped it round the old woman, and then ran home as fast as she could to make good the theft on her person before it was found out.

After about a year our correspondence slackened, and gradually broke down altogether. I heard from her once, perhaps, in six months. The tone of her letters struck me as altered. I could not say exactly how, except that it was more serious. She said nothing of archery meetings, or brushes carried off in triumph at the death, nor chronicled any feats of a similar nature. She talked about her family, and about mine, but said very little of herself. Once only, in answer to my inquiry as to what books she read, she told me that she was reading Father Faber, and read very little else. This was the only clue I gained to the nature of the change which had come over her. It was an exhaustive one. At the expiration of about two years a clergyman, who had been chaplain to her father for some time, came to Paris, and gave me a detailed account of the character and extent of the change.

The unceasing round of excitement into which

she had launched on returning home, and kept up with such unflagging energy, had, as might have been anticipated, told upon her health, never remarkably robust. A cough, which caused her family some alarm, set in at the beginning of the winter. She grew thin to emaciation, lost her appetite, and fell into a state of general debility. Change of air and complete rest were prescribed by the medical men. She was accordingly taken from one seaside place to another, and condemned to absolute repose. The system told on her so favourably that in a few months she was allowed to return home. But the monotony of a stay-at-home life, after the madcap career she had been used to, wearied her unspeakably. For want of something to do she took to reading, novels of course. Fortunately, ten years ago young ladies had not yet taken to writing novels that honest men blush to review, and that too many honest women do not blush to read. Mary did no worse than waste her time without soiling her mind. She read Dickens and Thackeray, and the good novels of the day, and if she was not much the better for it, she was probably none the worse. But one day—a day to be written in gold—a friend, the clergyman who gave me these particulars, made her a present of Father

Faber's *All for Jesus*. Reluctantly enough, Mary opened it, turned over the pages that promised little entertainment, and began to read. How long she read I cannot tell ; it might be true to say that she never left off. Others followed, all from the same pen, through uninterrupted days and weeks and months. She told me afterwards that the burning words of those books, the first especially, and the *Creator and the Creature*, pursued her even in her dreams. She seemed perpetually to hear a voice crying after her to arise and follow. Suddenly, but irrevocably, the whole aspect of her life was changed. She used to wonder, on looking back at the near past, whether it was she herself who had so enjoyed those balls and gaieties, or whether she had not been mad then, and imagined it all, and was only now in her right mind. The most insuperable disgust succeeded to her love of worldly amusements. She cared for nothing but prayer and meditation, or conversing with the poor, and tending them. An ardent longing took possession of her to suffer for and with our Divine Master. To satisfy this longing, and guided solely by the dictates of her new fervour, she began to practise the most rigorous austerities, fasting much and sleeping little, and praying almost uninterruptedly.

She had no director. During the last two years her spiritual life had been such a blank that direction had had no part to play in it. Under cover of her health, which, though now fairly restored, rendered quiet and prudence still desirable, she contrived to avoid all going out, and set herself a rule of life, to which she adhered religiously.

But this could not go on long. As she grew in the ways of prayer, the Spirit of God led her on to seek the only safe high-road for pilgrims aiming at a life of perfection and travelling towards the bourne of sanctity. The necessity for a spiritual director became clear to her, while at the same time the difficulty of meeting with this treasure, whom St. Teresa tells us to seek amongst ten thousand, grew more and more apparent and disheartening. Her father, a man of the world, very little versed in the mysteries of the interior life, but a good practical Catholic withal, saw the transformation that had taken place in Mary's tone and ways, and knew not whether to be glad or sorry. He acknowledged to her long afterwards that the first recognition of it struck upon his heart like a death-warrant; he felt it was the signal for a great sacrifice. She opened her heart to him frankly and unreservedly, seeking perhaps more at his hands than any father of mere flesh and blood could give; asking him to point out the road to her in which she was to walk, and to help her to tread it. That it must be a path of thorns in which she would need all the help that human love could gather to divine grace, Mary felt already convinced.

Her father, with the honesty of an upright heart, confessed himself inadequate to the task imposed on him, and proposed taking her to London to consult Father Faber. Mary, in an ecstasy of gratitude, threw her arms round his neck, and declared it was what she had been longing for for months. Father Faber had been her only guide so far. His written word had spoken to her like a voice from the Holy Mountain; what would he not do for her if she could hear the living voice itself, lay bare her soul at his feet, and have from his own lips the counsels she was struggling to gain unaided from his books!

They set out for London in a few days; but Mary was not to get there; the promise that looked so near and so precious in its accomplishment was never to be fulfilled. They had no sooner reached Dublin than she fell ill. For some days she was in high fever. The first medical men in the city, who were called in by the panic-stricken father, assured him there was no immediate cause for alarm, indeed no remote cause as the case then stood; the patient was delicate, but her constitution was good, and the nervous system sound, although rather shaken by the present attack, which was induced, they thought, by some sort of mental anxiety, together with a chill that had fallen on the chest. The event justified the opinion of the physicians. Mary recovered speedily ; but it was not deemed advisable to let her proceed to London. She relinquished the plan herself, with a facility that surprised her father, knowing, as he did, how ardently she longed to see Father Faber, and he could not refrain from asking her why she took the disappointment so coolly.

'It's not a disappointment, father. God never disappoints. I don't know why, but I feel as if the longing were already satisfied—as if I were not to go so far to find what I am looking for,' she answered, and quietly set about preparing to return home.

But they were still on the road of Damascus. On their way home they rested at the house of a friend near the monastery of Mount Melleray. I cannot be quite sure whether the monks were giving a retreat in the monastery, or whether it was being preached in the neighbouring town. As well as I remember, it was the latter. Indeed I doubt whether women would be permitted to follow a retreat within the monastery, and if not, this would be conclusive. But of one thing I am certain, the preacher was Father Paul, the Superior of la Trappe, in Ireland. I do not know whether his eloquence was anything beyond the common, judged, from a purely intellectual point of view; but many witnesses go to prove that it was of that kind whose property it is to save souls. To Mary it came like a voice straight from Heaven. She felt an imperative desire to speak to him at once in the confessional.

'I can give you no idea of the exquisite sense of peace and perfect security that came over me the moment I knelt down at his feet,' she said, in relating to me this phase in her vocation; 'I felt certain I had found the director who was to be my Father Faber.'

And so she had.

All that passes between a director and his spiritual child is of so solemn and sacred a character that, although many things which Mary confided to me regarding her intercourse with the saintly Abbot of la Trappe might be instructive, and would certainly be edifying to a number of interior souls, I do not feel at liberty to relate them. Even if I were not held back by fear of indiscretion, I should shrink from repeating these confidences lest I should mar their beauty, or convey a false interpretation of their meaning. When she spoke I understood her perfectly. When listening to the wonderful experiences of divine grace with which she had been favoured, and which she confided to me with the simple humility of a child, her words were as clear, and reflected her thoughts as luminously as a calm lake reflects the stars looking down into it and making the crystal mirror below a faithful repetition of the sky above. But when I tried to write down what she had said, it seemed to baffle me. There was so little to write, and that little was so delicate, so mysterious, I never seemed to find the right word to express it. When she spoke of prayer especially, there was an eloquence rising almost to sublimity in her language that altogether defied my coarse translation, and dissolved like a rainbow under the process of dissection. She was at home with the most elevated subjects, as if they had always been her natural theme, and the highest spirituality her natural element. The writings of St. Teresa and St. Bernard were familiar to her as her catechism, and she seemed to have caught the note of their inspired teaching with the mastery of sainthood. This was the more extraordinary to me that her intellect was by no means of a high order. Quite the contrary. Her taste, the whole bent of her nature, was the reverse of intellectual, and what intelligence she had, as far as any real culture went, was almost unreclaimed. Her reading had been of the most superficial, unmetaphysical kind; indeed her aversion to what she called 'hard reading' made her turn with perverse dislike from any book whose title portended instruction in the mildest form. She had never taken a prize at school, partly because she was too idle to try for it, but also because she had not brain enough to cope with the clever girls of her age and class. Mary was quite conscious of her shortcomings in this line; indeed she exaggerated them, as she was prone to do most of her shortcomings, and always spoke of herself as 'stupid.' This she decidedly was not, but her intellect was sufficiently below superiority to make her sudden awakening to the sublime language of mystical theology, and her intuitive perception of its subtlest doctrine, matter of great wonder to those who only measure man's progress in the science of the Saints by the gauge of human intellect.

'How do you contrive to understand those books?' I asked her once after listening to her quoting St. Bernard *à l'appui* of some remarks on the prayer of Union which carried me miles out of my depth.

'I don't know,' she replied, in her simple way, quite unconscious of having revealed any secrets of infused science to my wondering ears; 'I used not to understand them at all; but, by degrees, the meaning of the words began to dawn on me, and the more I read, the better I understood. Now, when I come to anything very difficult, I stop, and pray and meditate, till the meaning comes to me. It often surprises me, considering how stupid I am in everything else,' she continued, laughing, 'that I am able to understand spiritual books as well as I do.'

Those who have studied the ways of God with His Saints will not share her surprise. The life of the venerable Curé d'Ars is, in our day, amongst the most marvellous proofs of the manner in which He pours out His wisdom from the mouths of those who are counted by men as stupid.

But I am anticipating.

The meeting with Father Paul was Mary's first goal in her new career, and from the moment she reached it, she felt secure of being led safely to the end.

The intervening stages were, nevertheless, agitated by many trials: doubts as to the sincerity of her vocation, misgivings as to her courage in bearing up under the cross that was appointed for her, perplexity as to the direction in which that cross lay. While her lifeboat was getting ready, filling its sails and making out of port for the shoreless sea of detachment and universal sacrifice, she sat shivering, her hand on the helm, the deep waters heaving under her feet, the wind blowing bleak and cold, the near waves dashing up their spray, and the breakers far out roaring and howling at her in threatening clamour. There were rocks ahead, and all round under these foaming billows; sad havoc they had made of many a brave little boat that had put out from that port where hers was still tossing: home, with its sheltering love and care, piety enough to save any well-intentioned soul, good works to do in plenty, good example to give and to take, and the body not over-ridden with austerities against nature, not starved into despair, not exasperated by hunger and cold, and endless vigils, and prayer as endless. It was a goodly port and safe, this home of hers. Why should she leave it? See how the deep throws up its prey all round! Wrecks and spars and shattered remnants of bold vessels, and the lifeless bodies of their crew, are everywhere strewn over the waters. 'Take heed,' they cry to her, 'this is an awful sea; bold must be the spirit and stout and iron-clad the boat that tempts its stormy bosom. We came and perished. Would that we had never left the port!'

Mary never argued with the storm; but when it rose and beat upon her, she fell at the feet of Him who was sleeping in the boat below, and woke Him with the strong cry of humility and faith: 'Help me, Father, or I perish!' But when the waves fell, and the winds were hushed, there arose, ever and anon in the silence, a voice more ruthlessly terrible to her courage than the fury of ten thousand storms: her father's love. She was his eldest and his darling child. She had a brother and sisters too, all very dear. And cousins and close friends only less dear. She was a joy and a comfort to many. Must she go from them, and leave all this love, and the loveliness of life, for ever?

Mary's vocation, notwithstanding its strongly marked supernatural character, was not proof against these crucial alternations of enthusiastic courage and desolate heart-sinkings. Nay, they were, no doubt, a necessary part of its perfection. It was needful that she should pass through the dark watch of Gethsemane before going forth to climb the rugged hill of Calvary.

All this history she told me *a voce* when we met. In her letters, which were at this period very rare, and, at best, always very uncommunicative, she said nothing whatever about her interior life. A hard battle remained still to be fought with her father. It was long before her own faithfulness and his real piety triumphed over this obstacle. He had, from the first, vaguely acquiesced in her consecrating herself to God in a religious life of some sort ; but he believed, as every one else did, that to let her enter La Trappe would be to consign her to speedy and certain death. In vain Mary pleaded that when God called a soul, He provided all that was necessary to enable it to answer that call ; that her health, formerly so delicate, was now completely restored ; and that she had never been so strong as since she had lived in almost continual abstinence—(she never ate meat now on Wednesdays, Fridays, or Saturdays) —and that there were, moreover, *des grâces d'état* in the Conventual life which seculars did not dream of, and did not receive because they did not need them. In answer to these plausible arguments the incredulous father brought out the laws of nature and common sense, backed by the opinion of the eminent medical men who had attended her in Dublin, and under whose care she had been, at intervals, ever since. These men of science positively declared that it was neither more nor less than suicide for her to condemn herself to the unnatural life of the cloister, where want of animal food, added to the rest of the discipline, would infallibly kill her before the novitiate was out. Mary pleaded the supernatural against the natural ; but she pleaded in vain ; her father was inflexible. He went so far as to insist on her returning to society, and seeing more of the world before she divorced from it irrevocably. This check was as severe as it was unexpected. Her disgust for the vanities of her former life continued as strong as ever, while her longing for a life of immolation grew daily more intense, and more invigorating ; but humility made her tremble for her own weakness. How could she tell whether the strength which had borne her bravely so far, could withstand the attack of all the old temptations let loose on her at once? Her love of pleasure, that fatal enemy, seemed now dead; but only a short time ago it was an over-mastering tyrant; might it not rise up again into life, and, reinforced by the reaction prepared by the strain of her new life, attack her more violently and successfully than ever? All this was only too possible. There was nothing for it then but to brave her father, to set his authority at defiance, and save her soul in spite of him. She must run away from home.

Before, however, putting this wise resolve into practice, she consulted Father Paul. His answer was what most of my readers will suspect.

'Obedience is your first duty. No blessing can come from a breach of filial piety. Your father is a Christian. Do as he bids you. Appeal to his love for your soul, not to tax its strength unwisely. Then trust yourself to God as a little child trusts to its mother. He sought you, and pursued you, and brought you home when you were flying from Him; is it likely that He will forsake you now when you are seeking after Him with all your heart, and making His will the one object of your life? Mistrust yourself, but never mistrust God, my child!'

Mary felt the wisdom of this advice, and submitted to it in a spirit of docility, of humble mistrust and heroic confidence, and made up her mind to go through the trial as a test of the sincerity of her desire to seek God's will, and accomplish it in whatever way He appointed.

She had so completely taken leave of the gay world for more than a year, that her reappearance at a county ball caused quite a sensation. Rumour and romance had put their heads together, and explained, after their own fashion, the cause and motive of the sudden change in her life and her total seclusion from society. Of course, it could only be some sentimental reason; a disappointed affection, perhaps inadequate position or fortune on one side, a hard-hearted father on the other, &c. Whispers of this idle gossip came to Mary's ears and amused her exceedingly. As there was not a shadow of reality under the fiction, she could afford to laugh at it.

Her father, whose paternal weakness sheltered itself behind the doctors and common sense, did not exact unfair sacrifices from her at home. He allowed her to continue her ascetic rule of life unmolested, to abstain from meat as usual, to work assiduously amongst the poor, and to devote as much time as she liked to prayer. There were two Masses every morning in the village church, the first at half-past six, the second at half-past seven. He made some difficulty about her attending them at first. The church was nearly half an hour's walk from the house, and the winter morning, or night air as it really was, was likely to try her severely. But, after some arguing and coaxing, she carried her point. Long before daybreak she was to be seen on her way to the village. Her nurse, who was very pious, and devotedly attached to Mary, always accompanied her; not without objecting though. Every morning, as regularly as they sallied forth, Malone entered a protest.

'It's not natural to be gadding out by candle-light in this fashion, walking about the fields like a pair of ghosts. Indeed, darling, it isn't,' she would say to Mary.

Malone was right. It certainly was not natural; and if Mary had been so minded, she might have replied that it was not meant to be: it was supernatural. She contented herself by deprecating the good soul's reproof, and proposing to say the Rosary, to which Malone always assented.

So, waking up the larks with their matin prayer, the two walked on briskly to Mass. Once inside the church it was all right with Malone; set an Irish nurse to pray, and she will keep it up with any Saint in the Calendar. And Malone was behind none of the best; she was never loath to begin, but once on her knees and fairly wound up, she would go on at her devotions for ever; and when the two Masses were over and it was time to go, Mary had generally to stop her short in the full tilt of a Litany that the nurse went on muttering all the way out of church, and sometimes finished on the road home. But if she was ready to aid and abet Mary in her praying feats, she highly disapproved of the fasting ones, and more particularly of the long vigils which her young mistress imposed on herself. Mary confessed to me that the mastering of sleep was her greatest difficulty. She was by nature a great sleeper, and there was a time when early, even comparatively early, rising seemed to her the very climax of heroic mortification. By degrees she brought herself to rise punctually at a given hour; gradually, with the help of her Angel Guardian and a strong will, she brought it to five o'clock.

During this period of her probation her father took her constantly into society, to archery meetings, and regattas, and concerts, and balls, as the season went on. Mary did her part cheerfully. Sometimes a panic would seize her that the old spirit of worldliness was coming back—coming back with seven devils to retake her citadel by storm and hold it more firmly than ever. But she had only to fix her eyes on the beacon light and bend her ear to the life-bell chiming its *Sursum corda!* far above the moaning of the waters that were tossing their crested waves round her boat, and the foolish fears gave way.

No one who saw her so bright and gracious, and gracefully pleased with everything and everybody, suspected the war that was agitating her spirit within. Her father wished her to take part in the dancing, otherwise, he said, her presence in the midst of it would attract attention, and be construed into either censure or gloom. Mary acquiesced as regarded the square dances, but resolutely refused to waltz. Her father was satisfied with the concession, and did not coerce her further.

Things went on in this way for about a year. Father Paul, meanwhile, had his share in the probationary process. He knew that his penitent's health was far from robust, and, taking this into account, he endeavoured to attract her towards one of the active Orders, and used all his influence to induce her to try, at any rate, some Rule less austere than St. Bernard's before embracing it irrevocably. Animated by the purest and most ardent love for the soul whose precious destinies were placed under his guidance, he left nothing undone to prevent the possibility of mistake or ulterior regret in her choice. He urged her to go and see various convents, and make acquaintance with their mode of life. Seeing her great reluctance to do so, he had recourse to stratagem. He was anxious particularly that she should become acquainted with the spirit and rule of life of a community of Benedictines in X——, and, to compel her to do so unawares, he gave her a commission for the superioress, making many excuses for troubling her, and begging that she would only execute it when it was quite convenient to her.

Mary, never suspecting the trap that was laid for her, begged her father to take her up to the convent at once. The superioress, previously admonished by Father Paul, received her most affectionately, and, after discussing the pretext of the visit, invited her to see the chapel, then the house, and finally, drawing her into confidential discourse, explained all about its spirit and mode of life.

Mary, in relating this circumstance to me, said that although the superioress was one of the most attractive persons she had ever met, and the convent beautiful in all its appointments, she felt she would rather spend her days in the dangers of the most worldly life than enter there. The rule was not supernatural enough; the discipline not half austere enough, and she felt it would be impossible for her to make what she called a half and half sacrifice. Everything but La Trappe was unutterably antagonistic to her.

Father Paul, on hearing the result of his little ruse, confessed the truth to her. Noways discouraged, however, he maintained that she seemed to him much better fitted for a life of mixed activity and contemplation than for a purely contemplative one, and for a time forbade her to let her mind dwell on the latter as her ultimate vocation, to read any books that treated of it, or even to pray to be led to it. To all these despotic commands Mary yielded prompt, unquestioning obedience. She was with God like a child with a master; whatever lesson He set her, she at once set about learning it; easy or difficult, pleasant or unpleasant, it made no difference to her cheerful good-will. How few of us do like her! Instead of trying to learn our lesson docilely, we spend the school-hours in chafing over its difficulty, in dog-earing our book, and grumbling at the master; sometimes thinking, in our conceit, that the lesson is too simple, below our capabilities, and that we should do better something grander and more complicated. When the bell rings, we go up without knowing a word of it, and stand sulky and disrespectful before the desk. We are chidden, turned back, and set a fresh task. And so we go on from year to year, from childhood to youth, from youth to age, never learning our lesson properly; but dodging, and sulking, and beginning over and over again at the same point. How many are there who go on being dunces to the end of their lives when school breaks up, and they are called for and taken home—to the Home where the many mansions are, but none assuredly for the drones who have spent their school-time in idleness and mutiny!

To Father Paul, this spirit of child-like submission and genuine humility was more conclusive evidence of the solidity of Mary's vocation than the most supernatural favours would have been.

At last her gentle perseverance was rewarded;

grace triumphed over nature, and her father expressed his readiness to give her up to God.

In the summer of 1861 we were staying at V——, and it was there that I received from Mary the first definite announcement of her vocation. She wrote to me, that after long deliberation and earnest prayer and wise direction, she had decided on entering a convent of the Cistercian Order; and as there was no branch of it in Ireland, she was to make her novitiate in France. She had no idea where the *maison mère* was, and begged me to make inquiries, and let her know the result with as little delay as possible.

I will not dwell upon my own feelings on reading this letter. I had expected some such result, though it had not occurred to me, knowing the state of her health, that she could have entered so rigorous an Order as that of Citeaux. I had not the least idea where the novitiate was, and as the few persons whom I was able to question at once on the subject seemed to know no more about it than I did myself, for a moment the hope flashed through me that there might not be a convent of Cistercian nuns at all in France.

We had, on our arrival at V——, made the acquaintance of a young girl, whose name was

Agnes. My mother was already acquainted with her father and mother and other members of the family; but Agnes had been either at school, or more frequently absent amongst her relations for change of air, as she was in very delicate health, so from one cause or another we had never met till now. She was seventeen years of age, a fair fragile-looking girl, who reminded you of Scheffer's 'Marguerite.' Agnes had a young sister at the convent of La Sainte Enfance, not far from her father's residence, and she asked me to come with her to see this sister and a nun that she was very fond of. I went, and being full of the thought of my sweet friend in Ireland, I immediately opened the subject with the pretty talkative little nun, who came to the parlour with Agnes's sister.

'What a strange coincidence!' she exclaimed, when I had told as much of my story as was necessary. 'Why, we have at this moment a community of Cistercian nuns in the house here! Their monastery is being repaired, and we have permission from the bishop to harbour them in the mean time. See,' she went on, pointing to a couple of windows, whose closed *persiennes* were visible at an angle from where we were sitting, 'that is where they are lodged. You can speak to the prioress if you like, but of course you cannot see her.'

I was more struck by the coincidence than overjoyed at this speedy solution, which it promised, of my difficulty. I could not, however, but take advantage of the opportunity. Sœur Madeleine, as the little nun was called, ran off to ask 'notre mère's' permission to conduct me to the Cistercian prioress, and returned in a few minutes with leave to do so.

I was led to the door of the community-room, and through an extempore grating cut out of the panel, I held converse with the recluse. A few words acquainted me with Sœur Madeleine's mistake; her guests were not the daughters of St. Bernard; they were Poor Clares, an Order more rigorous even than the Trappistines; for, along with perpetual silence and fasting, it enjoins bare feet, except on a stone pavement or in the open air, when the nuns are obliged to slip their feet into wooden sandals. Of the Order of Citeaux the prioress could tell me nothing—nothing at least of its actual existence and branches, though she broke out impulsively into loving praise of its spirit and its saintly founder, and the great harvest of souls which he and his children had reaped for our Lord.

It was almost a relief to me to find there was no account of a *maison mère* of La Trappe in a quarter so likely to be well informed on the matter, and I began to hope again that Mary might be driven into some less appallingly austere Order from absolute inability to enter La Trappe.

I shall return to this angelic old prioress and to Agnes again. At present, as they do not further concern our narrative, we will let the curtain of that future hang.

Mary, meantime, had set other inquirers on the track of the Cistercians, and they had discovered that the novitiate was at Lyons.

After some preliminary correspondence with the prioress, the day was fixed for her to leave Ireland, and set out to her promised land.

She passed through Paris on her way.

It was three years since we had parted. I found her greatly altered ; her beauty not gone, but changed. She looked in much better health than I had ever seen her. Her spirits were gone, but there had come in their place a sweet serenity that radiated from her like sunshine. We went out together to do some little commissions of hers, and the better to escape interruption, for this was in all human probability to be our last meeting on earth.

We drove first to Notre Dame des Victoires, where, at her constantly recurring desire, I had been in the habit of having her name put down for the prayers of the Confraternity, and we knelt once more side by side before the altar of our Blessed Lady. From this we went to the Sacré Cœur, where Mary wished to see some of her old mistresses and ask their prayers. Perseverance in her vocation, and the accomplishment of God's will, were the graces for which she was incessantly praying herself, and begging the prayers of others. Her greediness for prayers was only equalled by her intense faith in their efficacy, and she never lost an opportunity of catering for them.

The *sœur portière* of the convent welcomed us affectionately; but when she heard that their former pupil was on her way to La Trappe, her astonishment was indescribable. If Mary had said she was going to be a Mahometan instead of a Trappistine, it could not have called up a look of more blank amazement than was depicted on the good sister's face.

The mistress of schools, and another nun who had been particularly kind to Mary during her short stay at the Sacré Cœur, came to the parlour. I did not assist at the interview, but Mary assured me they were almost as incredulous of her vocation as the *sœur portière* had been.

'It only shows what a character I left behind me,' she said, laughing heartily, as we walked arm-in-arm ; 'my turning out good for anything is a fact too miraculous for my best friends to believe in.'

It was during this long afternoon that she told me all the details of her vocation, which I have already narrated. She seemed transcendently happy, and so lifted by grace above all the weakness of nature, as to be perfectly unconscious that she was making any sacrifice. She was tenderly attached to her family, but the pangs of separation from them were momentarily suspended. Her soul had grown to the hunger of Divine love ; she had gone out into the desert where the manna fell, and, like the Israelites, she had fed upon it till all other bread was tasteless to her.

I expressed surprise at seeing her so untrammelled by human affections, and observed that this spirit of detachment would save her a great deal of suffering.

'O no,' she answered quickly, and with a sudden look of pain, 'it will save me none of the suffering ; that will all come later, when the sacrifice is made ;

but while it remains to be done, I always seem to have a kind of supernatural strength given me. I took leave of Father Paul and dear old Malone, and all the friends who flocked to say good-bye to me, almost without a tear; I felt it so little that I was disgusted with myself for being so heartless, while they were all so tender and so distressed; but when it was all over, and we had driven quite out of the road, I felt as if my heart was going to burst; I did not dare lift my eyes to take a last look at the old house lest I should cry out to them to take me back. And I know this is how it will be to-morrow.'

'And have you thought of the possibility of your being obliged to come home after all?' I asked.

'O yes; I have thought a great deal about it. It is quite possible my health may give way; it may be that I have mistaken the will of God altogether in entering La Trappe,' she replied, as coolly as if it were a matter of secondary importance.

'What a dreadful trial that would be!' I exclaimed. 'What a humiliation to you to have to come out after making such a stand about entering.'

She laughed quite merrily.

'Humiliation! And what if it were? I don't care a straw if I go into ten convents, and come out of them one after another, so long as I find out the right one in the end. What does anything signify but finding out the will of God?'

There was no mistaking the sincerity of her words. It was as clear as sunlight: the one thing necessary, the one thing that she cared a single straw about, was the knowledge and fulfilment of God's will. Human respect, or any such petty human motive, had got simply beyond the reach of her apprehension.

'And the silence, Mary?' I said, smiling at the recollection of her old school troubles and the tiffs with Mother Benedicta that she had told me of so often. 'How will you ever keep it? To me it would be the most terrible part of the Cistercian discipline.'

'Well, is it not odd?' she replied, stopping short, and laying her hand on mine impressively; 'it is so little terrible to me that I quite long for it. I keep repeating the words, *perpetual silence!* over and over to myself as if they were a melody. This was, I think, what decided me for La Trappe instead of Carmel, where they talk during the hour of recreation. It seems to me that complete hush of tongues must be such a help to union with God;

our tongues are always scaring away His presence from our souls.'

We came home to dinner. While we were alone in the drawing-room, she asked me to play something for her. She had been passionately fond of the harp, which she played very well, and stood by me listening with evident pleasure; when I was done, she went on drawing out the chords with her fingers in a sort of absent way.

'Does it not cost you the least little pang to give it up for ever, never to hear a note of music for the rest of your life?' I said.

'No, not now. I felt it in the beginning; but the only music that has a charm for me now is silence,' she answered—'perpetual silence!'

We parted. Never to meet again till we meet at the Judgment Seat.

On her arrival at Lyons the fatigue and emotions of the journey told on her. An acute pain in the spine, to which she was subject on the least over-exertion, obliged her to remain all day within doors at the hotel, lying down on a sofa. The following morning her father went with her to the monastery,* and gave her up to the prioress.

* It is dedicated to our Lady under the title of 'Notre Dame de toute Consolation.'

'I was less brave at the parting with my beloved ones than I ought to have been,' she wrote to me, 'but on account of the pain that kept me lying down in the midst of them all the previous day, I had not been able to spend much time in prayer, and so I had not got up enough strength for the trial time. I seemed to have let go my hold of our Lord a little, and to be leaning too much on them. The wrench was dreadful. . . . . But when I had been a few hours before the Blessed Sacrament, the pain calmed down, and I began to realise how happy I was. I am in great hopes that I have found the will of God.'

One trifling incident which gave innocent delight to Mary I must not forget to mention. She was asked, on entering, what name she wished to be called in religion, and on replying that she had not thought of one, and would rather the prioress chose for her, 'Then we shall call you Benedicta,' said the Mother; 'the saint has no namesake among us at present.'

The only disappointment she experienced in her new life was the gentleness of the rule, and the short time allotted for prayer!

It may interest some of my readers, and help them to appreciate the spirit of the novice, to hear something in detail of the rule which disappointed her in its severity. The Trappistines rise at 2 A.M. winter and summer. They proceed to choir, saying the Little Office of the Blessed Virgin. Then comes Meditation, chaunting the Divine Office, and Mass, followed by household work, which is distributed to each according to her strength and aptitude. Breakfast is at eight; but the rule relents in favour of those whose strength cannot carry them through so long a fast; these, and, if I am not mistaken, the novices in general, are allowed a little dry bread some hours earlier. The food is of the most frugal kind, but wholesome; excellent bread, vegetables, all descriptions of farinaceous food, fish occasionally, and good pure wine, are allowed at the principal meal, which is at three. The silence is perpetual, but the novices may converse freely with the mistress, and the professed nuns with the prioress. During the day they occasionally speak amongst each other by signs. They take open-air exercise, and perform manual labour out of doors. Indoors they work at church ornaments, vestments, &c.; some of the most elaborately wrought chasubles, Benediction copes, &c., used in the large churches throughout France, are worked entirely by the Trappistines of Lyons. They retire to rest at eight.

Mary described the food, and the bed, and the clothing, and all the details of the Monastic life as in every way delightful ; the digging, picking potatoes, &c., as most recreative, and not at all fatiguing. After her first Lent at La Trappe, she wrote to me that the 'time had passed so quickly she hardly knew Lent had set in when Easter came' Her only complaint was that the austerities, so mild during the rest of the year, were not sufficiently increased during the penitential season.

My third letter was on her receiving the habit. ' I wish you could see me in it !' she said ; ' I felt very odd at first, it was so heavy, but I soon grew used to this, and now it feels quite light and pleasant. I am so happy! I cannot help being almost sure that I have found the will of God.'

This was the burden of her song for evermore. To find the will of God ! And so in prayer and expectation she kept her watch upon the tower, her hands uplifted, her ears and her eyes, closed to all things else, straining night and day for every sign and symbol of that blessed manifestation. She kept her watch, never weary, faithful, ardent, growing in love, sinking more and more out of sight of self, deeper and deeper in humility. She had set her soul like a ladder against the sky, and angels were for ever hurrying up and down with the incense of her prayer, that no sooner reached the Throne than it dissolved in graces, and sent the angels flying earthward again.

The world went on ; the wheel went round ; pleasure, and folly, and sin kept up their whirl with unabating force ; all things were the same as when Mary Benedicta, hearkening to the voice from Sion, turned her back upon the vain delusion, and gave up the gauds of Time for the imperishable treasures of Eternity. Nothing was changed. Was it indeed so ? To our eyes it was. We could not see the changes that were coming of it, nor the work that her sacrifice was doing, nor measure the glory that it was bringing to God. Poor fools ! It is always so with us. We see with the blind eyes of the body the things that are of the body ; 'things invisible' we do not see. What do we discern of all the mysterious travail of humanity in God's creation ? The darkness and the pain ; little else. We see a wicked man, or a miserable man, and we are filled with horror and with pity ; we think the world is irretrievably darkened and saddened by the sin and the misery, forgetting the counterpart that we do not see : the sanctity of repentance and the loveliness of compassion. We see the bad publican flaunting his evil ways in the face of heaven, brawling in the streets and in the market-place. We do not see the good publican who goes up to the Temple, standing afar off, striking his breast, and sobbing out the prayer that justifies. We forget that fifty such make less noise climbing up to heaven, than one sinner tearing down to hell. So with pain. When sorrow overtakes a man, turning his heart bitter and his wine sour, we find it hard to believe that any good can come of it, that so much gall can yield any honey, so much dark let in any light. We cannot see—O, how it would startle us if we did!—what touching acts of kindness, what innumerable thoughts and deeds of love are evoked by the sight of his distress. They may not be addressed to him, and he may never know of them, though he has called them into life ; they may be all spent upon other men, strangers perhaps, to whom he has brought comfort because of the charity his sorrow has stirred in many hearts. Some miser has been moved by the story of his distress, and has opened his purse to that beggar at his own door. A selfish woman of the world has foregone some bauble of vanity and given its price to the poor. The example of his patient courage in adversity has been a solace and stimulant to others. There is no end to the small change that one golden coin of charity, one act of heroic faith, one chastened attitude of Christian sorrow, will send current through the world. It would be easier to number the stars than to count it all up. But the bright little silver pieces slip through our fingers unnoticed ; we do not watch for them. Neither do we hear the chime of the pure coin as it drops and rings all round us ; we do not listen for it ; we listen rather to the wailing and the hissing, hearkening not at all to the rustle of angels' wings floating above the din, nor to the sound of their crystal tears falling on the brine of human woe and sinful lamentation.

One more virgin heart is given up to the Crucified, one more victory is gained over the kingdom of this world, one more life is being lived away to God in the silence of the Sanctuary, and who heeds it ? Who sees the great things that come of it, the graces obtained, the blessings granted, the dangers averted, the temptations conquered, the miracles of mercy won for some life-long sinner, at whose deathbed, miles away, with the ocean perhaps between them, the midnight watcher before the Tabernacle has been wrestling in spirit with God ? Only when the Seven Seals of the Book in which the secrets of many hearts are written shall have been broken, will these things be made manifest, and the wonders of Sacrifice revealed.

Mary Benedicta was drawing to the close of her novitiate. So far her health had stood the trial admirably. She had entirely lost the pain in her back that she suffered so acutely from at home, and she had passed two winters without a cough, a thing that had not happened to her for years. Every day convinced her more and more that she had found her true vocation, and was 'doing the will of God.' Her profession was, finally fixed for the month of November. She wrote me a few lines announcing her approaching happiness, and begging me to get all the prayers I could for her. Her joy was the joy that passeth all understanding. It was too great for words.

I did not hear from her again, nor of her, till one evening I received a letter from Ireland telling me of her death.

Up to within two days of the date fixed for her vows she had been to all appearances in perfect health. She followed the rule in its unmitigated rigour, never asking, nor seemingly needing, any dispensation; she attended choir during the seven hours of prayer, mental and vocal, regularly every day; not one premonitory symptom came to warn the Community of any danger, when suddenly, at Matins one morning, Benedicta fainted away at her place in choir. They carried her to the Infirmary, and laid her on a bed. She soon recovered consciousness, but on attempting to rise, fell back exhausted.

Was this the summons? Yes. She was called for to go home. The Bridegroom was on His way to fetch her. A messenger was despatched in haste to the Archbishop for permission to solemnise her profession at once. Monseigneur Bonald granted it, and sent at the same time a special apostolic benediction to the dying child of St. Bernard.

Two hours later the chaplain of the monastery received her vows, which she pronounced in presence of the Blessed Sacrament and of the sisterhood assembled round her bed, weeping and rejoicing.

A little later, with a last effort of remaining strength, she dictated a few lines of loving farewell to her father. Then she was silent, calm, and rapt in prayer, listening perhaps to the joy-bells of Sion, and watching the golden gates that were slowly turning on their hinges. The day passed, and the night, and Benedicta was still waiting. At daybreak the Bridegroom came, and she went home with Him.

AGNES.

AGNES.

SHE was just seventeen when I first saw her; the eldest of five sisters. She was very pretty, but so spoilt by affectation that you quite lost sight of her beauty in vexation at her conceit. She seemed incapable of losing sight of herself for one instant; no amusement had power to distract her from observing the effect she was producing; self-consciousness amounted to a mania with her. If she went for a walk on the promenade, where the music, or any other attraction, drew a number of strollers to the spot, Agnes made herself a nuisance to everybody by the absurd affectation of her demeanour.

'People are looking at me! How dreadful it is! Let us go to some place where I sha'n't be stared at in this way. Did you see how that gentleman looked at me?' and so on.

It was true she was a pretty girl, and as such may have come in for more observation than a plain one; but the word 'grimacière' was written so legibly on her face and her person altogether, that I am satisfied most of the glances were directed to her less in admiration than in criticism. Anything and everything was a pretext *pour se mettre en scène*. If she saw children playing near the water, or sitting on the ledge of one of the fountains, she would clasp her hands, utter a little scream of terror, and beseech everybody to interfere, or else infallibly the little creatures would fall in, or fall over, and be drowned.

'There is not the remotest danger of such a catastrophe, and if there were, their mothers and *bonnes* are there to look after them,' some one would object; 'there is no reason for you to excite yourself about it.'

'True; but I am so sensitive! I have so much heart!' Agnes would answer, with a sigh, and, casting down her eyes, assume a new *pose*.

In fact, her life was a succession of *poses*, changing as place and opportunity suggested. Her temper, without being a bad one, was capricious, varying with her attitudes, and very disagreeable to live with; like all people who are too much absorbed in themselves, she was apt to be very forgetful of others. The only excuse that could be urged for the undisciplined silliness of her character and manner was her health, which had been so precarious and delicate from her cradle up as to render culture and restraint alike impossible. As a baby, she must not be thwarted in any infantine wilfulness, lest it should make her cry, and bring on convulsions. She had scarcely emerged from babyhood when she became a martyr to headaches that had never deserted her since. This furnished a pretext, not unreasonably, for emancipating her from lessons; and Agnes being, like the generality of human children, antagonistic to that bugbear of the nursery—her spelling-book—took the full value out of her headaches, and till she was quite a big girl could neither read nor write.

When she arrived at the age of fourteen it dawned upon her that she was a dunce, and that dunces, even when blessed with pretty faces, are not usually much admired or considered by their fellow-creatures. This discovery was unpleasant, and the remedy, though it was still in her hands, appeared to Agnes nearly as unpleasant as the evil. She hated study, and from not having had her mind gradually trained to the effort which it demands, even from the brightest children, before they take to it for its own sake, the simplest task was ten

F

times more irksome and difficult to her than it need have been. She tried to make up in some degree for lost time by applying herself to books at home; but the result was so inadequate to the labour that she soon gave it up in disgust. Two of her sisters had now been a year and a half at the Sacré Cœur, and they gave such pleasant accounts of their life there that, though the division of work and play struck her as too disproportionately in favour of the former to be thoroughly satisfactory, Agnes was tempted to try it. Her parents were delighted to let her make the experiment, and when her sisters were returning after the midsummer holidays they got everything ready for her to accompany them.

The trial was not very successful. Agnes was, of course, put into one of the junior classes, a position very mortifying to her vanity, and though the nuns, making allowance for the disadvantages under which she was placed, stretched indulgence to its utmost limits, she was not able to keep up with her little competitors. Her headaches, which, at first, owing probably to the change of scene and habit, had improved, grew more frequent and painful as the *trimestre* advanced, and, at last, the slightest mental exertion so palpably increased her sufferings, that she was obliged to leave. Disappointed and disheartened she resigned herself to being a dunce, and relapsed into her old life of idleness and inaction. Her health rallied after a while, and she again resumed the attempt at studying by herself. It was of short duration, however. Like many an older and more experienced student, she attempted too much, and failing, gave it all up in despair. Twice in the course of the following year she returned to the Convent, but with no better success than on the first occasion. So it happened that, at the age of sixteen, Agnes was as backward in the ordinary rudiments of knowledge as most children at ten. The only thing that gave any hope of her ultimately repairing the gap in her education was, that she had acquired a steady taste for reading. Even when her headaches prevented her from taking any part in the conversation, or remaining in the drawing-room when it was going on, she was able to read for hours in her own room, without apparently increasing the pain. Just when I became acquainted with her she was reading Racine, and used to talk with intelligent enthusiasm about his works and others that she had recently read. Her mind, hitherto a complete blank, seemed emerging at this period from its apathetic condition, and though she discovered no signs of talent, it was clear that she was not deficient in ability, and that she only wanted a fair chance to develop into a very intelligent woman.

She was exquisitely neat in her person, not extravagantly fond of dress, but paying a great deal of attention to it, and so very hard to please in the choice and fit of her clothes, that the maid who waited on her and her sisters used to say, that Mademoiselle Agnes gave her more trouble about her toilette than 'toutes ces demoiselles' together.

Her room was a pattern of neatness, and she took pleasure in making it look pretty with all sorts of nicknacks. In one corner she had a little altar, with flowers and candelabra surrounding a beautiful statue of the Immaculate Conception; on the wall above hung a large crucifix; and in front stood a priedieu, with a daintily embroidered cushion. Here Agnes performed her devotions; being debarred by her health from assisting regularly at daily Mass, she had taken pains to make her little oratory as complete and suggestive as possible; she was her own sacristan, and never allowed any one to assist her in the services it required. She had a tender devotion to our Lady, and without committing herself to *la vie dévote*, she was genuinely pious ; but her piety, though it was sincere, was not sufficiently active to control her character, and bring under subjection the inordinate love of notoriety, which made her so ridiculous, and, at times, so disagreeable.

However, taking her, with all her faults, she was a bright young creature, and inspired you with that sort of kindly superficial interest, which extreme youth, combined with no inconsiderable beauty, never fails to secure to its possessor.

One of her sisters, Jeanne, was at school at V——, at the Convent of the Sainte Enfance ; and Agnes, one morning, suggested that we should go and see her, and visit the Convent where she herself had spent a few months in one of her abortive attempts at getting educated. There was a nun also there whom she was very fond of, and went to see occasionally. This nun, Sœur Madeleine, I think, was her name, came to the parlour with Jeanne, and while the sisters chatted together over their little private affairs, Agnes relating all the home news to Jeanne, and Jeanne confiding her scrapes and fun and petitions for home to Agnes, Sœur Madeleine talked to me. I have related elsewhere[*]

[*] *Vide* 'Benedicta,' First Bell.

the subject that was engrossing my thoughts at that moment, and how startled I was, on mentioning it to Sœur Madeleine, to find that a community of Poor Clares were just then receiving the hospitality of the Sainte Enfance, while their monastery was being rebuilt. I had an interview, or, more properly speaking, an audience with the Abbess there and then, and having learned all I was anxious to know, had no idea of again renewing communications with her. Next day I was surprised to see Agnes arrive with a note to me from Sœur Madeleine, requesting that I would go and see her that afternoon before three o'clock. We both set off at once, not a little mystified by the summons, and losing ourselves all the way in conjectures as to what it could possibly mean. The explanation was very simple, though it was a great surprise to me. It appeared that soon after we left, the day before, the Bishop of the Diocese had come to visit the Poor Clares, and Sœur Madeleine, seeing how interested I was in learning all that concerned them, asked his Lordship permission for me to *see* the Abbess at the little monastery which she and the Mère Dépositaire were going next day to inspect before returning to it finally, and the Bishop had kindly granted the permission. We had half an hour to wait before they started, and I was glad to spend it in the garden with the Sœur Madeleine. The heat was overpowering. I recollect the day as one of the hottest of an exceptionally hot summer; Agnes and I were grumbling in our muslins, and pitying Sœur Madeleine in her black-stuff habit.

'Yes,' she said, laughing, 'it doesn't look very cool; but what is it compared to the habit of the Poor Clares? Theirs is as coarse and as heavy as a carpet. See, their windows are closed too; they do not give themselves the luxury of fresh air in the room that looks on the garden, because the noise of the children at recreation, and the voices of the visitors and people passing to and fro, would break the silence, and distract them at their meditations. *Notre Mère* went to see them a few days ago in the back room where they work. *Notre Mère* has permission. Well, only fancy, in this dreadful heat they had the window closed! *Notre Mère* nearly fainted when she went in, the room was so close; but thinking it was against their rule to open it, she said nothing. When she was going away, however, the Abbess went with her to the door, and in the humblest way asked her if it would be possible to have the window opened. The *espag-*

nolette was broken, or stiff, or something, and they could not turn it. You can imagine how vexed *notre Mère* was to find they had been suffering such an extra privation through our fault. She immediately sent up the gardener to arrange it, and the next time she went to see them, the Abbess thanked her as if she had done them the greatest favour, only they were afraid we had been scandalised at their self-indulgence in complaining about such a trifle ; but it was she who was to blame, the Abbess said ; she was afraid the novices might fall ill for want of air, but they had not complained. *Notre Mère* said she was as timid as a child, apologising for it, and so frightened that they had been a scandal to us. It makes us feel like Sybarites to see the life they lead.'

'It is a wonderful life,' I said. 'It sets one speculating whether they can have the same sort of souls to save, and the same interests at stake, and the same heaven in view as we common Christians, who take it all so easy.'

'O, yes, indeed it does,' answered Sœur Madeleine humbly. 'Even we, who have given up something in coming into the Convent, we feel so worldly, so luxurious beside them. It is a great privilege to be allowed to have them under our roof for a time, and we feel palpably that they are drawing down a blessing upon us. *Notre Mère* says she is quite certain that many graces which have been granted to us lately, and that we have been praying for for years, are entirely owing to their prayers. But it is no wonder; they are Saints; they must have great power with God.'

' Do you know anything of the previous history of any of them ?' I inquired.

'No; not even their names,' replied Sœur Madeleine. 'All we know of the Abbess is that she has been forty years in religion, and that she was twenty when she entered. She has one brother, who had never seen her of course since she took the veil. When the Poor Clares were going to leave their cloister she wrote to him to say that if he were here the day they moved he could see her, and they might embrace once more before they met in heaven. He was away in Spain when he got the letter, but he started off at once, travelled thirty hours without stopping, and arrived just as the Abbess was stepping into the cab; he caught her in his arms for a moment, and they kissed each other; then he let her go, and they parted without a word. He followed her here on foot to see the place she was coming to. *Pauvre garçon !* continued Sœur Madeleine, brushing away a tear, 'he found her greatly changed after forty years, though *notre Mère* says no one would believe she was sixty; she looks twenty years younger, and must have been quite beautiful ; her brother said she was ; he cried like a little child when he was talking to *notre Mère* about her. He went back to Spain next day.'

Agnes listened without a word of comment, but evidently with the deepest interest to all that Sœur Madeleine had to tell of their gentle saintly guests; and when the cab came to take the Abbess and her assistant to the monastery, she rose to accompany me after them. As I did not know the street, I took for granted she was coming merely to show me the way. It did not occur to me that she meant to include herself in my passport to the Sanctum Sanctorum. As we drew near the Convent, I discovered, however, that this was her intention.

'You won't be allowed in, Agnes,' I said ; 'the permission was only given for me.'

'O, I entreat you, let me go with you !' she exclaimed, in an imploring voice ; 'they will think we are sisters, and if you don't say anything they will let me in with you.'

I did not at all care to have her accompany me, and I could see no reason for her extraordinary eagerness beyond idle curiosity, and, perhaps, the perspective of a sentimental opportunity. I could not, however, refuse to let her take her chance.

The door was opened by a *tourière*. I made my speech, said I came by permission of Monseigneur, making no allusion to my companion. The Abbess had left word that I was to be admitted, and the *tourière*, as Agnes had counted, including her in the order, made no difficulty about letting us both in. The monastery was quite unfurnished; there was nothing but bare walls to be seen; but even these were invested with the mysterious interest that attaches itself to the Unknown and the Unseen. The rooms were small, and on the ground floor, with the exception of the chapel, there was nothing in them that differed materially from any ordinary house. The nuns, we were told, were up-stairs. Agnes and I ascended the narrow stair, she holding close to me, as if she were afraid I would escape, and leave her alone, outside the Presence Chamber. The Abbess came to meet us, however, and I introduced her at once, making the best apology I could for bringing her with me, and we both knelt down for her blessing. Then Agnes withdrew and left me alone with her. She took me round to look at the little there was to see, entering minutely and with great simplicity into all the observances of the rule.

The dormitory was a long room, cut up on one side into narrow strips of rooms by a lath and plaster partition, which did not ascend to the ceiling, but served rather as a screen to isolate the nuns in separate cells. There was not a chair or a bench to be seen; but in the centre of one room there were arranged a number of long sacks, that looked like monster gray sausages; they were filled with something that I fancied might be sand, they were so round and firm. The Abbess invited me to sit down on one of them while we continued our conversation. I did, or rather I tried; for the bag was stuffed so tight, and it was so round and hard and slippery, that it was quite a feat to maintain one's centre of gravity on it, and I kept constantly sliding down and pulling myself up again in the most uncomfortable manner. The Abbess noticed the difficulties under which I was labouring, and was distressed for me.

'You are very uncomfortable, my child?' she said.

'O, not at all, *ma Mère!*' I declared; 'but if it

is not an indiscreet question, may I ask what is so tight in these packed bags ?'

'They are our beds !' she answered, and laughed a sweet low laugh as an exclamation of horror involuntarily escaped me.

'How long do you sleep on them, *ma Mère?*' I asked.

'From half-past nine till midnight, and then from two till five.'

'Have you office during the two intervening hours?' I inquired.

'One hour of office and one of oraison. During this last we transport ourselves in spirit to all the places where at that moment our dear Lord is being most neglected and outraged, and we pray for the sinners who are offending His Divine Majesty, and we strive to console Him by our love. We call this exercise the hour of Gethsemane, in commemoration of the agony that oppressed His Sacred Heart when the sins of the whole world passed before Him, and when even His Apostles slept, and there was no one by to comfort Him.'

'And don't you sometimes fall asleep, *ma Mère?*' I said; 'it must be impossible to keep awake in perfect silence for a whole hour when one has been woke up out of a sound sleep?'

'In the beginning it is difficult,' she replied; 'the novices, especially the very young ones, have to fight hard to keep themselves awake; but they soon get used to it, and after a time it is the exercise they like best. It is such a beautiful thought—such a joy to feel that one is suffering a little for our dear Lord, and keeping Him company in His loneliness!'

There was a charm and a sweetness in her voice that are indescribable, and that made me long to look at her face—I could only see her mouth and chin, for the coarse serge veil concealed the upper part of it. The heat was so sultry that I wondered how she could breathe under such a weight of wool, and prompted really more by a desire to relieve her of it for a moment than from curiosity to behold her, I asked her if she would not raise her veil, as I had been told my privilege was to extend so far. She lifted it at once and went on talking. I was prepared by what Sœur Madeleine had said, to see the remains of beauty, but what I saw far surpassed my expectations. The skin was as white and almost as smooth as ivory; the mouth was chiselled; the nose small and sufficiently verging on the aquiline to give a touch of majesty to the face, whose delicately classic lines reminded you of one of the exquisite Vestal heads we sometimes see on cameos; her eyes were dark, but so limpid that, when the light fell full on them, they were as luminous as translucent gold.* The face was perfectly colourless, the lips alone relieving its ivory pallor by a faint pink glow. 'Notre Mère' was right: no one could believe the Abbess to be sixty years of age, and she was still very beautiful. After a few minutes she let her veil drop; it was evidently painful to her to remain uncovered, so I did not ask her to raise it again. She was deeply interested in all I had to tell about my friend whose vocation had led me to seek the acquaintance of the Poor Clares; and promised that she and the other sisters would pray for her with all their hearts.

The *Dépositaire* having overlooked every place, and given any instructions that were necessary for the final arrangements, now came to say it was time to return to their temporary home.

Agnes, who had been talking to her while the Abbess was engaged with me, was standing outside

* Once subsequently, but never before, the writer has seen this same peculiar lambent light in the eyes of a Carmelite.

on the landing, apparently waiting for me to rejoin her. I knelt down to receive the parting blessing of the Abbess, and then fell back to let her pass out before me. She did so, but stopped suddenly in the narrow doorway, uttering an exclamation of alarm or astonishment. I ran forward to see what was the matter, and beheld Agnes on her knees, clinging to the Abbess and sobbing convulsively. The Abbess laid her hand upon her head, and speaking to her with great tenderness, strove to raise her, or to elicit some explanation of her grief. But Agnes only sobbed and clung to her.

The Abbess in despair looked round at me. I felt satisfied it was all a piece of acting to make herself interesting in the eyes of the two nuns, and I felt very much inclined to say so and give her a good shaking. I controlled myself, however, so far as to look blank and mystified, and taking her by the hand I begged her to come away. After sobbing out an entreaty to the Abbess to pray for her, she was induced to rise and let me lead her down-stairs. Though I did not entertain a moment's doubt but that the sobs and tears were part of a scene got up from mere vanity and excitability, I was startled by the vehemence with which she played her part, and the reality of emotion that she threw into it. But this only exasperated me the more, because I saw the Abbess believed in the performance, and was distressed and frightened; so as soon as we were out of earshot at the bottom of the stairs I relieved myself by a suppressed burst of indignation.

'The idea of your making such a piece of work !' I said, 'terrifying those dear Clarisses in that way! You should not have forced yourself in on them if you could not control your feelings; though what there is in that sweet old Abbess to send any one into hysterics passes my comprehension!'

Agnes, without testifying the least resentment, pressed my arm, and struggled to keep down the sobs that were still choking her, but did not attempt to speak till we had helped the nuns into their cab, and it was off before us on the road. Then she said:

'I am very sorry; but I could not help it, indeed I could not. There was something in the voice of the Mère Abbesse, and in the touch of her hand when she laid it on my head, that seemed to break my heart, and make me feel as if I could never go away from her. O *chère amie*, how I wish I were a Poor Clare!'

I burst out laughing.

'Don't laugh!' said Agnes, not the least ruffled or affronted; 'I mean what I say; I would give everything I have this minute to be one. I would rather be a Poor Clare than a Queen!'

'I have no doubt you would,' I replied, 'and so would anybody in their right mind, if it could be done for the wishing; but when it comes to perpetual silence, and perpetual fasting, and midnight vigils, and walking barefoot, and being cased in a woollen carpet, and all the other ascetic delights that make up the reality of a Poor Clare's life, I think we are all safe to admire, rather than imitate it. And just see what a state you have put your eyes in!' I continued, looking at her swollen lids, and her face blurred with tears; 'what will they say at home when they see you?'

Agnes had quite forgotten this consequence of her emotion, and now it embarrassed her; she proposed instead of going straight home we should return to the Sainte Enfance, where she could bathe her eyes, and make herself a little presentable.

Sœur Madeleine sent her off to the lavatory, and then appealed to me for an explanation of the tears. She shook her head when I had related the episode with the Abbess.

'I was provoked out of all patience with her,

ma Sœur,' I said ; 'and then the idea of her carrying on the comedy with me, and talking about being a Poor Clare !'

'Yes,' said Sœur Madeleine, 'and the worst of it is that this constant *mise-en-scène* that she indulges in makes it next to impossible to know what is genuine in her feelings from what is not.'

'But you do not think that any part of this was genuine ?' I said, 'that she was suddenly seized with a vocation to the Poor Clares ?'

Sœur Madeleine hesitated, and raised her shoulders with a dubious shrug.

'One can never tell,' she said after a pause ; 'the law of vocations is so altogether mysterious and supernatural. *Si le bon Dieu voulait—*'

'O, *si le bon Dieu voulait*, He might work a miracle,' I acquiesced, laughing ; 'but do you think Agnes at all a likely subject for such a miracle as that, *ma Sœur ?*'

'No, I certainly do not ; but I think that if she ever did become a nun, it would more likely be in an out-and-out austere Order like St. Clare's, than in one like ours, for instance. She is a strange child ; I had her under my eye for two months, and I watched her closely ; I think she has immense capabilities for good, and if once she were roused to exert them, there is no saying what might come of it. *Et puis, voyez-vous,*' she added, with a singularly expressive look, ' *elle aime beaucoup la Sainte Vierge, cette enfant.*'

We left V——, and returned to Paris. It was six months before I again saw Agnes. She wrote to me occasionally, and generally mentioned the Poor Clares, in whose chapel she assisted at seven-o'clock Mass every morning latterly. I was glad to hear this, because it argued a great improvement in her health; but the circumstance never struck me as foreshadowing anything more important. Soon after she told me of it her mother came to see us, and I was surprised to hear that her headaches, instead of being better, were quite as bad, and at intervals even more distressing than formerly. I alluded with astonishment to her being able to go to daily Mass at such an early hour.

'I don't know how it is,' replied her mother, 'but she says it does not fatigue her; of late she seems to have more energy in fighting against pain; she is somehow changed altogether; her character has, as it were, entered on a new phase, and shaken off the childishness that had clung to it up to the present; it has taken a much more serious turn. The little vanities that she used to attach so much importance to, have lost all their charm for her; and the only thing she seems to care for in the way of amusement is reading.'

I learned from others more minute particulars about this change in Agnes's character and tastes. Everybody who saw her was struck by it. The restless longing for notoriety that had hitherto been so manifest had quite disappeared, and given place to a dignified modesty that added a charm to her beauty as much as to her manner, and won her, now that she had ceased to court it, all the admiration she had formerly been so eager to attract.

It was not many months after this visit of her mother's, about a year from the date of our acquaintance with Agnes, that a great change took place in the worldly affairs of her family. Up to the present she and her sisters had been brought up with the certain prospect of handsome fortunes; nothing was spared on their education, and they were allowed a latitude of expense in other ways in keeping with the expectations of the daughters of a man of large and secure income; the elder girls dressed, not extravagantly, but with an elegance that necessitated rather formidable milliners' bills; their habits altogether were luxurious; and they had never been taught to consult economy in any department. With these tastes and antecedents they were badly fitted to meet and grapple with the altered fortunes that were in store for them. Their father had involved himself in large financial speculations for some time past ; they were, as so often occurs in similar cases, brilliantly successful at first, and fully justified his somewhat rash and sanguine anticipations ; but the failure of an important house concerned in them consequently checked their career ; and, one fine morning, Monsieur X—— woke up to find himself a bankrupt, and his children beggars. Although for more than a month he had foreseen such a catastrophe as all but inevitable, he kept the knowledge a profound secret even from his wife. She noticed his careworn looks with some anxiety, but never dreamed of attributing them to their real cause ; thought he was tired and wanted change—anything rather than the truth—and so, happy in him and in her children, she lived on, unsuspicious of the gathering thundercloud that was about to burst over her little paradise. It did burst. But it did not crush her. Instead of reproaching her husband with the misfortunes which had brought ruin and desolation upon her and her children, instead of upbraiding him for the want of frankness which had led her on blindfolded and unprepared to the very edge of the gulf, she roused all her energy to meet the demand upon her fortitude, to sustain her husband, and to ward off the first bitterness of the blow from her children. She had passed for rather a commonplace character in her easy-going days of prosperity; but in this hour of trial the wife and the mother rose up in all their strength and tenderness, and asserting themselves with the majesty of self-devotion, transformed the woman into a heroine. Those who knew her best were startled at the way in which she revealed herself, as much as by the prompt intelligence she displayed in confronting the position of her affairs. She made herself at once acquainted with every detail of the circumstances. From beginning to end her husband had acted with unflinching integrity. He had wronged himself and his children; but he had, intentionally, wronged no one else; even if material evidence had been wanting to this effect, the spirit in which he accepted his disaster was sufficient proof of it to his wife. Their ruin was complete. Nothing remained of his own ample fortune, and only a small pittance of Madame X——'s *dot*, which happened to have been so placed by marriage settlements as to make it unavailable for the risky investments in which the rest had been swamped, was rescued from the wreck. This would still enable her to keep her children in the very humblest way at home; but there was of course nothing left for the expenses of education. This she resolved to undertake herself, and assisted by Jeanne, who was now sixteen, very intelligent, a good musician, and for their age very well educated, she hoped to make up to the little ones for the advantages from which they had been prematurely cut off. Madame X—— talked over all this with her husband, looking the prospect boldly in the face, and reducing all their hopes for the future to practical schemes for the present. He, manlike, was too stunned by the blow at first, and too despondent to look beyond the disasters of to-day; but when she told him he would rally soon, and then with his natural ability and education, and influential connections, be sure to obtain some honourable appointment, either at home or abroad, which, if it did not replace him in the position he had lost, would at least enable him to live and to make some provision for the children, he listened to her, trying to believe it, and yielded himself up to her guidance with the passive confidence of a child.

But this woman, who was so brave for him, and so heroically forgetful of herself, was a coward for her little ones. She could not bring herself to tell them the truth. From day to day she put it off, on one pretext or another, always resolving that to-morrow she would speak to them ; but to-morrow came and found her as irresolute as yesterday. After all there was no hurry ; better wait a little. There was a seizure in the house ; all their costly furniture, the precious household gods, were to go in the general wreck ; but it would not be till the end of the month, the creditors had mercifully granted that delay, and she could prepare the children meantime gradually to hear the truth. The midsummer holidays were at hand when Jeanne and her sister would be home, and this would furnish an excuse for an excursion to some distant place, where they would start on their new life of poverty and toil amongst strangers, and so escape the humiliation of outstaying their bankruptcy in the place where they were all known.

More than a week elapsed, and the children were still in happy ignorance of the terrible break-up that was threatening their young lives ; they went on in the usual way, practising and working, and making their little picnics into the neighbouring woods, enjoying the innocent pleasures of the day, and sleeping the happy dreamless sleep of their age.

It was for Agnes that both her parents feared most; her health had always been so delicate, how would it withstand this shock? She who had been nurtured like a hothouse plant, sheltered so tenderly from every breath of wind and every shadow of fatigue, how would she bear the life of privation that was before her? Her father, who had maintained an attitude of passive endurance under every other menace of the future, broke down before this one, and when alone with his wife gave way to passionate grief and self-reproach on account of Agnes.

'Courage, *mon ami!*' Madame X—— would say to him, with a cheerfulness that her heart belied; 'let us trust in God. She has a Father in heaven who loves her better than you; He will take care of her.'

A fortnight dragged on; the plan of a journey to the south had been discussed before the children, and joyfully approved of, as any plan promising change and excitement was always sure to be. Hints were then thrown out that it might be found necessary for them to remain in the south, that certain losses which their father had sustained lately in money matters might make it impossible for them to come back and go on living as they were, &c. But the truth foreshadowed in this abstract way made no deep impression, and was far from exciting any alarm in their minds. The days went on, and they drew nearer and nearer to the crisis when a revelation of the whole unvarnished truth was inevitable, and still Madame X—— shrank from speaking out. More than once she had taken Jeanne and Agnes for a walk by themselves with the intention of talking to them on the subject, and each time her heart, with motherful cowardice, failed her.

Things were in this state, when, early one morning, the Marquise de —— came to pay Madame X—— a visit. This lady was spending the summer at V——, with her son, a young man of six-and-twenty, who was heir to a large fortune, and the idol of his mother. After some preliminary conversations on indifferent subjects, Madame de —— began to speak of Agnes in terms of the greatest admiration. She praised her beauty, her modesty, which lent such an additional grace to it, her gentleness, her piety, till Madame X—— was at a loss for words to deprecate the eulogy with becoming humility. When she had exhausted herself in praises of Agnes, the Marquise entoned those of her son. No mother ever had such a son, or ever could have; he had never given her a moment's pain or anxiety;

he had every virtue under the sun, and not a single fault; he loved his home; he had no tastes that were not refined, no pursuits that were not ennobling, no companions who were not honourable and well-conducted.

'In fact,' said the Marquise, bringing her panegyric to a climax, 'if I were not his mother, Madame, I would say that my son is a pearl!'

Madame X—— was a Frenchwoman; she knew as well as Madame de —— what this double panegyric was meant to preface, and what was the motive of this early visit. Alas! if it had been only a month ago, how gladly she would have hailed such an offer for her child! How radiantly she would have responded to the Marquise's graceful encomiums on Agnes; how warmly she would have echoed those she lavished on her son! But they fell cold on her now. They could avail nothing. Agnes was a portionless girl—a bankrupt's daughter; if the Marquise knew this, she would no more think of offering her son to her than of making her family a present of half her fortune. Why should she? Would Madame X—— do it in her place? No mother in France would. Madame X—— almost wished the Marquise had known the truth, and not forced her to the painful alternative of either seeming to slight her offer, or having to expose her own misfortunes. She made some complimentary remarks on the excellence of the young Marquis's disposition, and congratulated his mother on having such a son; then, intending to give the conversation a more general turn, she observed that although girls were a great comfort, they were an immense responsibility, and that she had often wished it had pleased God to give her a son. This last remark was either wilfully or accidentally misunderstood by the Marquise, who exclaimed quickly, holding out her hand to Madame X——,

'He offers you mine, *chère Madame;* take him, and give me Agnes in exchange.'

Madame X—— was at a loss what to say.

'You do Agnes, and all of us, a great honour by such an offer,' she said at last: 'and I wish it were possible for us to accept it; but Agnes is so young —much younger than most girls of eighteen; her health has kept her back in every way. I fear she would not be at all a suitable wife for your son.'

'That is for him to decide,' said the Marquise, laughing; 'he does not object to it, being somewhat in the same predicament himself; it is a defect they will get cured of together; and, besides, it is not any given number of years, or their equivalent, that a young man looks for in a wife, so much as good principles, amiability, and charm ; and where will he find all this better than in Agnes ?'

'Her youth is not the only obstacle,' persisted Madame X——; 'the disparity between her fortune and your son's is great—greater than you suppose. We have lived hitherto in a way that has altogether misled you on this point.'

'It is one to which myself and my son are completely indifferent,' said Madame de —— emphatically ; 'his fortune is large enough for himself and his wife, and he has no desire to increase it. Albert has always had a horror of what we call *un mariage d'argent.*'

'He is an exception to all the young men of his day,' observed Madame X——, with a sigh.' 'O, if this had but come a month since, Agnes might have been his wife now, and—'

'He *is* an exception,' repeated the mother proudly ; 'and so is Agnes ; they are made for each other ; let us not place imaginary obstacles in the way of a union that has in itself every element of happiness.'

'Would that they were imaginary, or that any act or sacrifice of mine could overcome them !' exclaimed Madame X——; and, unable to control her feelings, she burst into tears. Soon recovering herself, however, she bluntly told the Marquise that owing to recent embarrassments they were not in a position to give one fraction to their daughter on her marriage.

'That is perfectly immaterial to us,' observed the Marquise, with a contemptuous wave of her hand.

Madame X—— was in despair.

'Chère Madame,' she said, 'your generosity forces me to an avowal which, for my husband's sake, I would have suppressed, if possible: he is at this moment a bankrupt! We have lost everything, and our children are beggars!'

'I know it; I know all,' answered the Marquise.

'And knowing all, you still—' Madame X—— stopped, astonishment choked the words in her throat.

'I still ask you to give me Agnes for my son.'

Madame X—— could not command her voice to answer, but she held out her arms to the Marquise.

The two mothers embraced and wept together for a moment in silence.

'I know everything,' resumed Madame de ——, after their emotion had relieved itself in tears; 'I have known it from the first. Your misfortunes are less of a secret than you imagine; but you would not regret it if you knew what universal sympathy they have inspired, and what admiration and respect are felt for your husband's honourable conduct, and your own resignation and courage.'

Once the ice was broken, it was a relief to Madame X—— to unburden her heart of the anguish that had been pent up in it so long without the solace of friendly sympathy, and to find that their misfortunes, instead of being an obstacle to Agnes's making a happy and brilliant marriage, had been the means of hastening its accomplishment.

Madame de —— informed her that her son, who had seen Agnes several times in society, in church, and out walking, had been very much struck by her; so much so, that two months ago, on coming out of the Cathedral, where, to the detriment it is to be feared of his own devotions, he had watched her during Mass, he told his mother that if he were inclined to marry, that was the girl he would like. This admiration grew every time he saw her; but though opportunities were not lacking, the habits of French society prevented his taking advantage of them to acquaint Agnes with his feelings, or attempt to win her good opinion. His mother, who believed her younger than she was, did not particularly encourage Albert in his fancy; she did not oppose it, however, only advised him to wait till he had seen a little more of the world, and a greater variety of eligible young ladies. Agnes was safe not to be run away with for a year to come, and if, at the end of that time, he still preferred her to any one else, he should have her blessing and consent to his marriage. But before three months had elapsed, total ruin had overtaken the X—— family The Marquise was one of the first to hear it, through a friend who was himself considerably compromised in the disaster; but she heard at the same time how nobly the bankrupt father had behaved, how regardless he had shown himself of his own interests, till the interests of those who had trusted him were secured. His wife's conduct was beyond all praise, and while it inspired admiration for herself, it drew additional sympathy round her husband. No one felt more sincerely for the brave-hearted mother than Madame de —— did; but when her son announced his determination to marry the bankrupt's daughter without further delay, she protested. Such an alliance was not to be contemplated for the Marquis de ——. It was very noble of Albert to think of it, of course, and his mother admired him for it; but it was her duty to stand between him and such a boyish freak of romance. To her astonishment, Albert, for the first time in his life, rebelled. He declared that he loved this penniless girl; that he would marry her, and win a claim to her gratitude by placing his fortune at her feet in time to rescue her family from ruin; if his mother loved him and valued his happiness, as she professed to do, instead of thwarting it now that it was within his reach, and making him miserable for the rest of his life, she would assist him in obtaining it, and go, without further delay, to make an offer of his hand to M. and Madame X——. The rebellion lasted for three whole days, during which time it was a question which of the two was more miserable, the mother or the son. On the morning of the fourth day, Madame de —— acknowledged herself in the wrong, and, yielding to the generous and reasonable arguments of the young lover, surrendered unconditionally. Having once laid down her arms as an antagonist, she took them up as an ally, and that very hour set off to plead his cause with Agnes's parents. We have seen with what result.

As soon as everything had been explained between the two ladies, Madame de —— requested her friend to go for Agnes. She did so; but here, in the quarter where she least expected it, a powerful antagonist lay in wait.

I have already mentioned the marked change which had come over Agnes, and if I have not dwelt upon it in detail, it arises from the fact that no incidents occurred to emphasise the change which could afford material for narrative. It was not the circumstances of her life that were altered, but its colour and tone. The first idea of a religious vocation, which had revealed itself in that hysterical scene at the Poor Clares, had gradually grown and strengthened, till the thought grew into desire, and desire into determination, and an ardent longing for the perfect life possessed her soul, haunting it night and day. As yet, she had not spoken of it to any one, for though the resolve was deep and firm, it was still undefined as to the exact time for carrying it out. That morning, however, during her thanksgiving after Communion, the impulse came upon her so strongly that, unable to resist it, she pledged herself to its execution for the following Sunday, made the offering of herself to our Lord, and promised to dedicate her life to His Cross as a daughter of St. Clare.

She came home, intending to acquaint her mother with what she had done, and request her to break the intelligence to her father and her sisters. But when she found herself in the midst of them all again at breakfast, the effort which, in the illuminated strength of prayer, had seemed so easy, assumed a strangely different aspect. The cross which had lain so lightly on her an hour ago was weighted now to agony, and instead of seeking her mother at once, as she had intended, Agnes escaped to her own room, and spent the morning alone, bracing up her courage for the coming ordeal. On her knees, with her crucifix in her hand, she was strong ; but the moment she stood up her courage sank. She remained, therefore, almost uninterruptedly in prayer, fighting against her own heart, and wrestling with God in her weakness.

When Madame X—— opened the door she was startled at the almost ecstatic fervour of the young girl's attitude, as she knelt, not on the prie-dieu, but on the ground beside it, her hands clasping her crucifix, and her head bowed on her breast. The mother saw no vision of angels hovering above her child, she caught no echo of the seraph choir, 'harping on their harps' the canticle of that white-robed virgin train who follow the Lamb whithersoever He goeth ; she only saw that Agnes was bathed in a halo of modest loveliness that surpassed anything she had ever seen before, and a thrill of innocen motherly pride quickened her heart at the thought that if her child had neither gold nor silver, she had yet a dower that was more precious than both.

'Agnes!' said her mother softly.

Agnes looked up, but instead of rising to meet her, she stretched out her hand to Madame X——, and motioned to her to come and kneel down beside her.

'Let us say a prayer together, mother,' she said.

Madame X—— knelt down, and giving utterance to the emotions that were overflowing her soul, she gave out the first verse of the *Magnificat*. Agnes was struck by the selection of the song of praise so admirably suited to her own feelings at that moment, and answered every alternate verse with an exultant fervour, that seemed to her mother like a prophetic response to the glad tidings she was about to announce.

'He who is mighty has indeed done great things for you, my child. Let us give Him thanks with all our hearts,' exclaimed Madame X——, rising from her knees, and embracing Agnes, while tears of gratitude streamed down her face.

Perplexed by this preface, and not conjecturing

in the remotest degree what it portended, Agnes listened in silence while her mother related the joyful news. When they were told she remained perfectly silent, betraying neither astonishment, nor pleasure, nor distress.

Madame X——, mistaking her silence for timidity, or the over-fulness of heart, natural on so solemn an occasion, smiled, and caressing her tenderly, 'Come, now,' she said, 'and embrace your new mother; she is waiting for you, and she is prepared to receive and love you as a daughter.'

But Agnes, instead of obeying her, stood still and dumb, rooted to the spot, looking at her mother as if she had not heard her, or understood the import of her words. Then, rousing herself, and speaking in a voice of strange solemnity,

'Mother, it can never be,' she said; 'I can never be a daughter to Madame de ——, or her son's wife; I am betrothed already.'

Madame X—— drew back, and only answered her by a look of bewilderment.

'Yes, mother, I am betrothed. I can have no other spouse than Jesus. I am going to be a Poor Clare.'

'A Poor Clare!' repeated Madame X——, after staring at her for some time in dumb astonishment; 'a Poor Clare! In Heaven's name, what do you mean by this folly?'

Agnes entreated her to sit down, and hear what she had to say. The story of her vocation was soon told, from that first meeting with the Abbess, which Agnes felt to be her destiny, till the definite act of renunciation which she had made that morning during Mass in the little Chapel of St. Clare.

Madame X——'s first thought was, that Agnes, in some accidental way, had learned the state of her father's affairs, and that, shrinking with natural horror from the life of poverty, and perhaps toil, that was before her, and for which she was in every way so ill-adapted, had resolved, under the first impulse of grief and humiliation, to fly from it, and seek shelter in a convent; there, at least, if the material sufferings were greater than any she could be exposed to at home, they would be compensated by the sense of voluntary sacrifice, and by those unearthly joys and spiritual consolations which, seen through the mystical haze of the cloister, assumed, to Agnes's over-wrought and ardent fancy, the fascinating proportions of the supernatural, and were magnified into the visions and raptures of the Saints.

'My child,' she said, with gentleness, but with

an air of grave authority, 'if, under the influence of excitement, you have made any rash vow, its very rashness invalidates it; you did wrong, under any circumstances, to pledge yourself to such a step without proper counsel and direction, and without asking and obtaining the consent of your parents. If you were prompted to it by cowardice, by a reluctance to accept the cross which God, in His wisdom, has seen fit to lay upon us, you yielded to a temptation of the enemy. And do you think that God would accept, or bless a gift offered from such motives? That He would approve of your rejecting the cross of His choosing to take up one of your own? And should you persist in taking it up, do you suppose He will furnish you with the superhuman grace and strength necessary to persevere in carrying it?'

'I don't understand you, mother,' replied Agnes quietly; 'I have nothing to shrink from in life that I know of, and with the exception of my health, which I cannot leave behind me, I have never had a cross of any sort.'

The look of innocent surprise with which she said this convinced Madame X—— quite as much as her words that Agnes had heard nothing. Her vocation to the Poor Clares was clearly neither prompted nor superinduced by cowardice or by despair. In one sense this was a relief; but, on the other hand, it revealed a resolution deeper and more matured than Madame X—— wished to believe in. The occasion was ripe for telling Agnes the truth concerning their reverses, and her mother availed herself of it, not, indeed, gladly, but more willingly than an hour ago she would have believed possible. She laid the cruel facts before her: their ruin was complete; nothing remained but a pittance, just enough to give them all bread; the sale of their furniture, &c., was to take place at the end of the month; by special consideration for Monsieur X—— the creditors had put it off till then, in order to give him time to rally from the blow, and make the necessary preparations for the departure of his family. Where were they to go? How were they to live henceforth? These were the questions that had been knocking at her heart ever since the day when the disclosure of their ruin made it necessary for her to discuss the future. For herself the poor mother cared little; but she carried in her heart the superadded sorrows of her children, foretasting with exquisite sensitiveness every privation, every pang, every humiliating consequence of the poverty that was before them.

Through the weary watches of the night she had cried out to the Father who is in heaven to have pity on her little ones, and to let the burden of His justice fall not upon them, but upon her ; and He had heard the cry, and mercifully sent her help and comfort in the way she had least expected it.

Agnes heard the terrible story to the end, and then sat silent, like one in a dream. *Ruin, disgrace, beggary !* And she might save them from it all, and she could not. She must not. Truly, God had smiled upon the sacrifice which, but a few hours ago, she had laid at His feet ; for, lo ! He had sent down fire from heaven to consume it. He would have it a holocaust, a whole burnt-offering ; her heart, with all its capabilities of agony, with every sublime renunciation, every human bond and privilege and reward, must be gathered together in one relentless grasp, and flung into the sacramental flame. For one moment her soul was paralysed. A mist of doubt and strife and admonishing fear encompassed her ; her eyes grew dim ; she lost sight of Calvary, and the everlasting hills beyond, where the Bridegroom crowned for the marriage feast sat waiting for her, and she saw nothing but a lamentable waste, full of emptiness and darkness and despair. But it was only for a moment, enough to make her soul go up in a loud cry for help against itself. Then she was rescued ; the glance of Jesus fell upon her heart, and hushed its terrors, and chased away the darkness.

She was inexpressibly pained and shocked ; but the idea of being false to God, and betraying her vocation for even the best and purest human consideration, she felt was inadmissible, and she said so.

Her mother, at first incredulous, now grew pale with indignation.

'What !' she cried, ' will you be so heartless to your sisters, so ungrateful to your father and to me, as to reject a marriage that will be the salvation of us all, for the sake of following out a fanatical delusion of your own ? At the moment when we were driven to despair, and knew not which way to turn, Providence sends us a plank in our shipwreck, and you, from a freak of sentimental piety, you fling it from you, and let us all sink, rather than renounce your own stubborn will. Agnes, it is impossible you can be so cruel !'

Agnes wept as if her heart would break, and, falling at her mother's feet, declared she was ready to make any sacrifice on earth to prove her love and duty to her father and to her. If she were fit to help in the education of her sisters, or to gain anything for them by working at her needle, or if she had bodily strength to help in the labour of the house, which must now fall almost entirely upon themselves, she would recognise it as her duty to stay with them and bear her share of the common burden ; but, as it was, she could only add to it. She was too ignorant and too delicate to be of the slightest use in any way, and, as to the contracting a marriage which, under the circumstances, she felt would be little short of sacrilege, going straight against the will of God, and imperilling the salvation of her immortal soul, Agnes declared that no consideration on earth would ever constrain her to it.

Finding reproaches and severity unavailing, and not being in a mood just then to take up another weapon which might prove more effective, Madame X—— rose, shook herself from the embrace of the sobbing girl, and bidding her ask for light to see her wickedness and folly, returned to the *salon*, where the Marquise was impatiently waiting for her. She explained the cause of her absence, treating Agnes's refusal on the grounds of a religious vocation as a childish chimera, which a few days' sober reflection would suffice to dispel. Madame de —— was inclined to look at it more seriously ; it might, indeed, be only a passing 'exaltation,' but it might be something more; in any case, she doubted its being so rapidly disposed of as Madame X—— seemed to expect.

'Let me see her,' she said; 'take me to her room, and leave us together for a little.'

Madame X—— did so.

The Marquise found Agnes still weeping and agitated, but calmer than when her mother had left her. They remained closeted together for nearly an hour.

Madame X——, who was waiting in nervous expectation for the result of the long conference, was somewhat relieved to hear that Agnes had consented to go and spend a week with the Marquise at her country place.

'I am to call for her myself to-morrow,' said Madame de ——; 'in the mean time, don't argue with her, and, above all, don't scold her. My impression is that we may conquer eventually; but it will not be by threats or by entreaties. It must be a matter of time. I will do my best, at any rate. She is worth it,' added the Marquise; 'she is a prize worth fighting for.'

Madame X—— was more alarmed than reassured by the anxious tone in which she made these remarks. Clearly, the conquest of this vocation, real or imaginary, which had so inopportunely started up between Agnes and the fairest earthly prospects, would be less easy than she had supposed.

Prompted by her own heart, as much as by the parting advice of the Marquise, Madame X—— sought Agnes in her room once more, and folding her to her heart, asked her in the tenderest language to forgive her her recent harshness, expressed full confidence in her love and obedience, and promised to urge her no further on the subject, but to leave her to the dictates of duty and affection.

The Marquise came next day, and carried away Agnes. Her mother's anxiety during the ensuing week can be more readily imagined than described. She wearied Heaven with prayers for the success of the marriage, which would prove such a blessing to all her children, and, for the moment, every other thought and care was suspended, or merged in this all-absorbing one.

Meantime, Madame de—— made good use of her opportunities. Her son was with them at ——, and, by the most delicate and respectful devotion of his demeanour towards Agnes, seconded his mother's duel with St. Clare. He did not make love to her. In every word and act he carefully avoided all that could scare her sensitive timidity by seeming to do so; but he pleaded his cause in a language more persuasively eloquent than any words could have been. Fearing that his presence *en parti tiers* might embarrass the young girl, or seem like an unfair pursuit, Madame de —— had invited a few near relatives to spend the week with them at the château. They knew why they were bidden, and, touched by their cousin's disinterested boyish love, as well as by Agnes's youth and beauty, they took a kindly interest in the issue of the little romance, and did their part of cousinly courtship by treating her very affectionately, and showing by their manner that they would make her welcome as one of the family.

But it was all too late. Another Bridegroom had come, and pleaded, and Agnes had given her heart to Him, and she could not take it back. There was a struggle; not to renounce the bright prospects that were spread out before her in such alluring guise, but to inflict the pain of the renunciation upon others. This was the temptation that Madame de —— laid hold of and worked with unrelenting assiduity. Would it not be a nobler kind of sacrifice to forego her own desire, to renounce the higher life of mystical union with God for the sake of those beloved ones to whom she owed so much? Was she likely even spiritually to lose by so doing, and would not God repay her sacrifice by granting her in the married state all the graces and helps towards sanctification that awaited her in the monastic life? To all this Agnes would answer with quiet unvarying iteration: 'He that loveth father and mother better than Me is not worthy of Me.'

'When I repeat this,' she said one day to Madame de —— as they were walking together on an elevated point that overlooked the valley where the picturesque old château with its park and winding river lay in luxuriant beauty at their feet, 'when I repeat the same words, Madame, I feel as if it were not I who said them, but some one else in me; I can't help wondering how it is that neither your kindness, nor Monsieur Albert's, nor this beautiful place that I admire so much, nor the thought of the happiness my marriage would bring to them at home, seems to touch me even as a temptation! I feel as if I were not really here, but some one else in place of me.'

Madame de ——, who had started on her mission rather in passive acquiescence with her son's wishes than moved by strong desire for its ultimate success, had been at first stimulated by Agnes's opposition, and gradually won by her gentleness and goodness, till she had set her heart upon winning her almost as ardently as Albert himself.

But the Marquise was a Christian, and moreover, what is not always synonymous even amongst good Catholics, she believed firmly in the doctrine of vocations. When it became clear to her that Agnes had a vocation to the religious life, she ceased all opposition, and mentally resolved to fight the young girl's battle if necessary against the family, and even against Albert.

Before Agnes left them, Albert, by his mother's permission, had a walk with her alone, and for the first and last time pleaded his cause openly and ardently. Agnes was distressed, but not the least frightened at this, to a French girl, most extraordinary and unparalleled proceeding on the part of a *prétendant;* she repeated what she had so distinctly said to his mother, thanked him with unabashed simplicity for the kind feelings he had expressed towards her; and asked him to think of her as a sister, while she would remember him always, and pray that he might be happy with a better wife than she could have made him.

Thus ended the visit which might have proved a pitfall to a less solid vocation, but which served only to confirm that of Agnes, and to convince those who had striven to shake it that 'she had chosen the better part,' and that it was in vain to try to take it from her.

She turned her back upon the fine old place, and the broad lands, and the loyal young heart to whom her presence there would have made his home a paradise, and relinquished all without so much as guessing that she had made a sacrifice.

One week later Agnes knocked at the door of the little monastery which, just a year ago, we had visited together, and asked to be admitted amongst the daughters of St. Clare.

For three months after her entrance her headaches increased, and continued with unabated violence. Day or night she had no respite. Then suddenly they ceased, never to return; and with them disappeared every trace of the debility that had made her life, from childhood up, so irksome that it had been little better than a sustained effort. The rule, which had few terrors for her in the distance, lost all its bitterness when she embraced it, and lay as lightly on her as a silken mantle. The perpetual silence; the bare feet without even a sandal between them and the ground; the unbroken fast; the broken sleep; the long hours of mental and vocal prayer on bended knees; the monotonous round of infinitesimal duties in the novitiate; Agnes found it all sweet and light and beautiful.

A friend who went to see her, or rather to hear through that dreadful black screen of St. Clare's—a sheet of iron perforated with holes not bigger than a pin's head—asked her if she did not find the rising at midnight very hard :

'O, no,' said Agnes, laughing, 'on the contrary, I enjoy it ; it rests one from the bed !'

Any one who had sat upon a Poor Clare's bed could readily believe that this was indeed the fact.

During the whole term of her novitiate she was never once obliged to accept a dispensation. When the time was fixed for her profession, she wrote to me announcing it, and describing her happiness in terms that would sound like exaggerated romance if they referred to the most perfect earthly bliss; but which were no doubt inadequate to express the foretaste of that bliss which it has not entered into the heart of man to conceive. She alluded with playful simplicity to the day when we had gone together to her present home, not reproaching me for my rude and stupid misconception of her outburst of emotion on beholding the saint-like old Abbess who was destined to be her spiritual mother, but thanking me with enthusiastic gratitude as having been the instrument of so great a gain, the beginning of such a happy end to her.

So, in the sweet spring-time of her girlhood, Agnes, who had rejected the flowery garland of an earthly bridal, crowned herself with the crown of thorns which the Poor Clare wears on the day of her nuptials with the King of Heaven. She wears the outward symbol for that day only; but what is her life evermore but a prolonged commemoration of that mystery of the crown of thorns?

I never saw her again but once, and that was in a dream. The clouds rolled back, and through the open glory poured a flood of light and song; angels, bearing lilies in their hands, let down a silver ladder from the sky; below, a virgin, lily-crowned, and robed in garments like the snow, and holding in her hand a lamp that shone like a saphyr star, stood with arms outstretched; and the angels trooping down exultant, with a voice like the voice of many waters, bore her up the ladder, and the Bridegroom, crowned and beautiful, and shining like the sun, came forth to meet her. Then the clouds rolled back once more, the echo of the seraph's alleluias died away, and the glory faded from the sky.

ALINE.

ALINE.

WE were talking about miracles the other evening, and some one remarked that a miracle was like a ghost—everybody knows somebody who has seen one, but nobody ever sees one himself.

'I beg your pardon,' I said, 'I have seen one.'
And I told the story, as I now write it.
God gave me a friend once. She was French. Her name was Aline. She was married at twenty. I did not know her then; but she told me the story of her marriage years after, and used to laugh heartily at my insular wonder at the prosaic manner in which the affair was conducted. She went to spend the evening at the house of a lady where a number of young friends of hers were in the habit of going once a week, taking their work or their music with them, and holding a little *salon* of their own at one end of the room, while their elders conversed, or sat round a card-table at the

other. On this particular evening, a gentleman dropped in rather late; and, after paying his respects to the lady of the house, and conversing with some of the guests whom he knew, took leave, without having once addressed Aline, or any of her young companions, or, as far as they could see, even cast a glance to that end of the room. She, however, noticed his air of distinction, and wondered who he was; but it was a mere passing curiosity, and she had ceased to think of him before she returned home. Next morning her mother, who was called Madame André, to distinguish her from a sister-in-law, came into her room, and, after embracing her, said, with emotion,

'My child, thy grandfather and I have been much preoccupied of late concerning thy future. He is old, and I am not growing young, and my health is far from robust. All this makes it desirable that thou shouldst find a protector as speedily as possible. M. —— whom thou didst see last night has made an offer for thy hand. He is all that we could desire in a son-in-law.'

And she proceeded to enumerate the advantages which the gentleman presented, and ended by telling Aline to think over all this, as they gave her until the next day to make up her mind.

'I don't want an hour, *ma mère*,' said Aline unhesitatingly. 'Since you are satisfied on the essential points, that is enough for me. I noticed M. —— last night, and I was greatly struck by his *distingué* manners and appearance; so if I have had the good fortune to please him, he also pleased me.'

And without any preliminary romance, the marriage was forthwith arranged. If you are unacquainted with French manners and customs, this matter-of-fact way of proceeding will probably shock you a little; but the system works very well abroad, and, though I am far from advocating its adoption for home use, I must say in fairness, that these cool business-like unions turn out, very often, quite as happy as those contracted under more poetic conditions in our own more romantic land.

Aline's experience certainly tells strongly in favour of the prosaic system. Never was there a happier married life, a union more complete and tender than hers. Her husband was a man of high principle, strong affections, and refined and cultivated tastes. He was magnificent in his liberality, and a prince in his charities; so much so that the poor people nicknamed him 'M. le Prince,' and the *sobriquet* was caught up by his friends, who familiarly called him by it. Aline used to complain that he entered so quickly into her charitable schemes, sometimes even forestalling them, that she never had a chance of showing off her eloquence, and 'carrying a point,' as other wives boasted of doing with reluctant husbands. He, on his side, complained that she never had a fancy for anything, and would look at the prettiest trinkets in a jeweller's shop without longing for one of them.

'Say if I am not to be pitied,' he would say to his mother-in-law, 'to be married to a woman who never has a caprice!'

There was one fear that hung like a cloud over Aline's happy life, one sorrow that, on her bridal day, she had prayed to be spared above all others. She dreaded being left a widow. The sight of Madame André's agony after her husband's death had made such an impression on her as a child, that for years she secretly determined never to marry, and thus avoid the possibility of incurring a like misfortune; and from the moment of her marriage, she prayed every day of her life to be spared it.

For seven years it seemed as if the prayer were to be heard. M. ——'s health was excellent, and never gave his wife a moment's concern. But suddenly there came a change; alarming symptoms showed themselves, and increased so rapidly, that soon it became plain to every one, except Aline, that the days of her earthly happiness were numbered. She, however, remained blind to the danger. Everything that science could do was done; watering-places were resorted to, systems were tried, all to no effect. She saw this, and yet she continued blind. The idea that her husband was going to die did not, apparently, present itself to her as a possibility. She either could not, or would not, see it. Any other sacrifice she was ready to make—her children, her health, her fortune, one or all of these she was ready to give up without a murmur. But her husband! that was a sacrifice not even to be contemplated. She had somehow, by dint of praying against it, made up her mind that God would never ask it of her, and it now seemed as if no warning, short of death itself, could shake this belief. She besieged Heaven, meantime, with prayers for the restoration of his health; she could not go beyond this form of petition; but if God willed that it should never be restored, and that he should remain an invalid for the rest of his life, she was perfectly ready to accept the decree.

M. —— grew so ill at last, that it became

merely a question of time, and the medical men ordered him to remain in Paris for the winter, in order that close attendance and medical skill and care might do what was still possible to prolong life and alleviate his sufferings. Even at this crisis, Aline refused to see the danger.

'My last words to her at parting,' said her mother, 'were, "God send you strength to bear whatever He sends, my child!"'

'Yes, mother,' replied Aline, in her emphatic way, 'that is what I ask Him with every breath I draw. But not that! God is merciful. He *knows* that cross would be heavier than I could bear. He won't send it to me.'

It was a long illness; ten months, I think. Alice tended her husband through it with a love 'passing the love of woman.' She never left his bedside day or night, grudging the attendant sisters even those laborious offices that were beyond her own frail strength. When the doctors entreated her to leave the hot sick-room for an hour, and go for a drive or a walk, she replied—and it was true —that she felt no want of rest or of fresh air. When they urged the risk to her own health by this prolonged confinement and fatigue, she smiled in an amused way. What better use could she make of her health than to spend it in her husband's service? They pleaded her children, to whom her life was precious; but she could not think of her children, of any one or anything but the one beloved life that was telling away its treasure, day by day, before her eyes.

The hour of the supreme sacrifice came at last. Her husband died like a Christian. He had loved the poor, and gave up his soul in humble peace to Him who has made our mercy to them the measure of His mercy to us.

Madame André had been with the children in the country all this time. As soon as the end came, she started for Paris.

'I can give you no idea,' she said, relating the history of those days to me long afterwards, ' of the kind of terror I had of meeting Aline. I could hardly believe that, if I found her alive at all, I should find her in her right senses. I thought of how she used to shudder at the bare mention of the sorrow that had now become a reality; how often I had heard her protest her willingness to accept any other sorrow, to make any other sacrifice, if only this one were spared her; that she *could* not give up her husband! And now that the cry had been answered, as those passionate cries so often are, by the rejection, I shrank from meeting her like the veriest coward.'

It was late at night when Madame André reached Paris. She had been travelling since morning, and was exhausted in mind and body when she rang at her daughter's door. It was opened at once, and before the servant could answer her breathless inquiry, 'How is your mistress?' Aline herself appeared. They embraced in silence, and neither spoke until they entered the drawing-room, when Aline turned to give some orders to the servant about refreshment. She spoke with great calmness; there was no tremor in her voice, not a tear, nor the trace of one, in her eyes. When they were alone, Madame André said, looking at her in a kind of awe,

'My child, it has not crushed thee!'

'Crushed me! No, mother. How could it, when God's arm was between me and the blow?' Then, taking her mother by the hand, she led her into an adjoining room. There he lay, stark and silent. It was consummated, the one sacrifice that her whole life had recoiled from. They knelt down and said the *De Profundis* together. It was all as simple, as calm, as if they were performing some ordinary devotion, solemn and sacred, but devoid of all bitterness or terror. Madame André felt as if she were in a dream; nothing was real but the supernatural, and that was so near, so vivid, that it made the material fact seem dreamlike.

The body was conveyed on the following day to the country, to be interred in the family vault. Throughout the journey, which lasted ten hours, Aline preserved the same extraordinary composure, scarcely shedding a tear, absorbed either in silent prayer, or else reciting aloud the Office of the Dead, the Rosary, or other indulgenced devotions.

Several members of the family were at the station to meet her. She greeted them with a serenity that bewildered, while it moved them to tears.

The coffin lay that night in the village church. Soon after daybreak next morning, Madame André went into Aline's room; but there was no one there. Madame André, guessing where she was, hurried out to the church. There she found Aline kneeling beside the coffin, with her cheek resting against it in a half-caressing attitude that was indescribably touching. Her tears were flowing unrestrainedly. After returning her mother's embrace, she lifted her head, and looked at her with the strangest expression. 'Mother,' she said, 'I wish I could tell you what I feel. I know that life is over for me; that all my happiness is buried here'—laying her hand softly on the coffin—'and yet—I cannot describe it—but I feel as if my heart were *breaking* with gratitude to God for the way in which He is sustaining me! The sense of His goodness is absolutely joy! While I live I never shall forget the mercies of this hour!'

Nor did she. The pledge thus given while the flood was sweeping over her was faithfully fulfilled. Gratitude to God and a prevailing sense of His goodness continued an abiding sentiment with her, and thanksgiving was henceforth her favourite devotion.

But the strong hand which upheld her so sensibly in those first days of her bereavement, was gradually and for a season withdrawn, and Aline was left to struggle on through the desolation of nature unaided, in order to learn that highest lesson of the Cross, entire dependence on God, and utter mistrust of self. But these struggles which she underwent in the solitude of her heart remained a secret between herself and God; He was their only witness; it was to Him only that she turned for consolation, in His ear alone that she uttered her complaint. When her heart brimmed over, prayer was the cup that received its overflowing.

Her life, in course of time, resumed outwardly its habitual activity and even brightness; she never, indeed, regained the brilliant mercurial kind of gaiety which had exercised such a fascination over all who knew her in her happy days; but her spirits were always bright, and lent a wonderful charm to her society.

She prolonged the period of deep widow's mourning as far as was consistent with the limits of custom and the feelings of those around her, and then quitted it for a kind of unostentatious second mourning of violet and gray to which she adhered to the end of her life.

Her three little girls were now her chief interest and occupation, and she devoted herself to training and educating them with characteristic energy, studying their faults and qualities, their tastes and abilities with the utmost care, and bringing all the resources of her rare intelligence to deal with the character of each. For their sake she consented to take proper care of her own health, which hitherto she had systematically neglected, spending herself on every occasion with a sort of prodigal self-devotion. From the moment that she came to realise

K

that her mission henceforth was the forming of these little immortal souls, the terror of dying before the charge was fulfilled, took possession of her, gradually growing into an *idée fixe*, just as the fear of her husband's death had formerly been. Madame André, meantime, watched this sympton with an anxiety that soon took the shape of a presentiment, as in the case of the once dreaded widow-hood. Aline by degrees worked herself into the belief that God had in some way pledged Himself to avert the calamity of her death, and to leave her on earth until her children were safely embarked in life, and no longer in need of her. She began to talk in the old way of her complete submission to the will of God on every point, except this one; she could not die because she had a mission to fulfil, and our Lord, who had given her the mission, knew that, and would leave her until it was accomplished.

Her health, meantime, began to cause considerable uneasiness to those around her; she had never recovered the strain put upon it by her arduous attendance on her husband during his long illness, and she was now paying the penalty of those ten months' fatigue. She suffered from constant and agonising headaches, acute internal pains, and a weakness that amounted almost to the loss of the use of her limbs; she could only walk for a few minutes on perfectly level ground, and had to be carried up and down stairs. These premonitory symptoms did not, however, open her eyes in the least. The medical men talked vaguely about neuralgia, nervous debility, and so forth, and, failing to see any definite or organic cause, treated her for an ordinary case of rheumatism or neuralgia, with exhausted vitality. They sent her about from spa to spa, ordering baths and waters, and trying a variety of experiments, none of which afforded the slightest relief. Two years were spent in this way; but Aline, now in the condition of a complete invalid, was still blind to all sense of danger, and confirmed in the belief that she was safe to live until her children no longer needed her.

What she underwent, meantime, with their education, and what she made others undergo, it would fill a book to tell. They were being educated from morning till night. It was a favourite theory of their mother's that seculars ought to have a sound knowledge of theology, that in these days, when infidels are armed *cap-à-pie* with weapons of reason and sophistry, Catholics ought to have adequate scientific knowledge of dogmatic theology to enable them to cope with their enemies, and 'render an account of the faith that is in them.' 'It is not enough to teach children their catechism in days like ours,' she was fond of repeating, 'they want something more; they ought to be sufficiently grounded in doctrine to give an answer to the whys and the wherefores of unbelievers.' Acting on this principle, she invited a devout and learned ecclesiastic to instruct her children in the whole range of Catholic doctrine, and he came to her house twice a week for this purpose.

Then there were the music-lessons. O! that music, what a purgatory it was to every one concerned! Aline carried her peculiar originality more daringly, perhaps, into this department than any other. When she herself was about twelve years old, she was taken one evening to hear a celebrated violoncellist. It was the first time she had ever heard the instrument, and its effect on her was startling; she described it as like the sensation of having some fluid poured through all her veins, and waking a new sense within her. She listened, spellbound, while the music lasted, and then stole across the room to her mother, and whispered in her ear:

'*Ma mère*, let me learn that; give me a violoncello!'

The tears were in her eyes, and she was trembling from head to foot.

Madame André, who was the most intelligent, as well as the most indulgent of mothers, discerned the revelation of a gift in the child's extraordinary emotion, and promised to think about it. She gave her a violoncello, and a very few lessons sufficed to show that she had done wisely. Aline, who had so far displayed but mediocre ability on the piano, soon promised to arrive at excellence on the nobler instrument. She had a beautiful voice, not powerful, but of penetrating sweetness, and her small exquisite figure suited well the picturesque violoncello, on which she always accompanied herself. Her husband, who was very proud of his wife's artistic talent, used to declare she had selected the violoncello with an eye to effect, and to the display of her hand and arm, both of which were, indeed, fitted to serve as models for a sculptor.

But whatever little complacency she may have taken in these gifts as a young girl and a wife, it was all over now; everything of the sort was sacrificed the moment she became a widow. She never sang, except to her children in the nursery, and the beloved violoncello was laid aside until her eldest daughter was old enough to begin music. Then

Aline presented it to her. She could not, however, endow her with the spirit which had inspired the bow in her own hand.

The second sister chose the violin, and the piano fell to the lot of the youngest. What the mother had now to endure under the purgatorial dispensation which she had thus erected about her ears I shall not attempt to describe. The violin and violoncello went on for two hours a day each, and the piano for one hour, and as all three performers were in the most rudimentary stages of their respective instruments, it is easy to imagine the combined effect. It must have been torture to Aline's highly sensitive musical organisation, and yet she was never once seen to wince under it, nor to evince anything but delight in the hideous discord. Even when, at last, she was confined to her bed, and suffering intense pain, the strumming and scraping went on just the same on every side of her. What was more surprising still was the indifference with which she inflicted this misery on her mother. Madame André suffered from chronic liver complaint, and was subject to sick headaches that made her morbidly sensitive to noise of any sort; Aline felt acutely the annoyance which the practising caused her mother at these times; but what was to be done? The children must practise. Hers was the tenderest, most unselfish nature I ever knew; but where anything connected with her children was concerned, no tyrant could be more merciless.

The only thing that divided her time and interest with her three little girls was the service of the poor. She had all her life devoted a large portion of her leisure to active labours amongst them, and when ill-health made this no longer possible, she organised a system of charity to be carried on by others under her guidance and with her money. She founded an asylum where a certain number of orphans were taught and clothed, and then either started in life as servants, or, as Aline much preferred, when this was possible, as married women in humble homes of their own.

I must mention one characteristic incident connected with this foundation. It was to be conducted by the Sisters of St. Vincent, but on an original plan of Aline's, and she was requested to draw up a little book of rules wherein her views and intentions should be clearly defined. She had a great horror of 'drilling' children into piety, and wished that, as much as possible, prayers and outward practices of religion should be the result of their spontaneous devotion, the outcome of their education rather than its form. There was probably a tinge of exaggeration in this as in many of her theories. However, she drew up the rules, setting forth forcibly her opinions on the point and on the system of education generally which she considered best fitted to children of this class. It was a delicate and responsible task, and Aline prayed long and fervently before undertaking it; once begun, she threw all her spirit into it, and spent considerable time and thought in its accomplishment. She then placed it in the hands of her director, a wise and excellent man, and gave him *carte blanche* to alter, curtail, or add, as he thought fit. The abbé perused it carefully, and returned it to her with a few words of discreet, but warm approval. But it so happened that he met Madame André the same day, and to her he spoke unreservedly. 'It is a *chef-d'œuvre* of the interior spirit; there are pages here and there that read like extracts from St. Teresa; they are positively inspired!' Madame André, with the innocent indiscretion of maternal pride, went straight with this report to the author. Aline flushed up slightly, and turned off the subject; but her mother was naturally curious to see the work which had called out so magnificent a eulogium from competent authority, and recurred to it presently. Aline still turned it off, and on one pretext or another delayed giving her the MS. for several days. At last, driven into a corner by Madame André's persistency, she was obliged to confess that she had destroyed it. The abbé's praise had roused a feeling of self-complacency in her, and she resolved on the spot to commit the cause of it to the flames. The eloquent treatise was soon after replaced by a short summary of rules and regulations whose composition offered no scope for literary display.

The history of this little orphanage would furnish in itself an interesting chapter; but I must content myself with merely mentioning its existence as an evidence of Aline's intelligent and practical charity. The digression, however, tempts me to make another. My friend had been about two years a widow when there occurred an episode which, though she herself played a subordinate part in it, is too striking to be omitted in this brief sketch of her life. She had a friend, a widow like herself, but whose bereavement was stripped of those blessed consolations which had sustained Aline under hers.

M. X—— had been nominally a Catholic; but his faith, like that of too many Frenchmen, was purely theoretical; he had given up the practice of religion since his boyhood, and beyond accompanying his wife to Mass on Sunday, he never set foot in a church. Otherwise, he was the most estimable and amiable of men, upright, truthful, charitable, a model husband and father. Madame X——, on the other hand, was looked upon by those who knew her as a kind of saint. This absence of all practical faith on her husband's part was a thorn in her heart, and she never ceased praying and getting others to pray for his conversion. She had great devotion to the Stations of the Cross, and performed them daily for this intention. But she had now been married many years, and M. X—— showed no sign of change on the one point where it was needed. His wife, meantime, fell into bad health, and the doctors advised him to take her to a watering-place in the south. They were staying there at an hotel, and one day at the *table d'hôte* (as well as I remember) the conversation turned on religion, and a gentleman present thought fit to make some blasphemous remarks on the divinity of our Lord. M. X—— immediately fired up as at a personal insult, and burst out into an eloquent defence of the divine mystery, betraying in his countenance and manner a singular warmth of emotion. The bystanders were variously affected by the *sortie;* some were edified and touched, others amused. Soon after this M. X—— left the room and went to take his bath. While in it, he was seized with a fainting fit, and on the door being unlocked, he was found dead in the water. His wife's feelings can be imagined only by those who have had to mourn a loved one under somewhat similar circumstances. It seemed at first as if her reason must give way under the twofold sorrow of the shock. To her it was not merely a temporal but an eternal death. She saw her husband lost for ever, and mourned him as one who refused to be comforted. A person who had been present when M. X—— had defended the mystery of the Incarnation a few hours before, exclaimed, on hearing of her state of mind, ' What ! Does she not remember how almost with his last breath her husband defended the divinity of Jesus Christ ? and have we not our Lord's own word for it, that those who confess Him before men, He will confess Himself before His Father ?'

This was repeated to Madame X——, and brought her wonderful consolation ; the words sounded like a message from the other world. Still, though she never relapsed into the first state of despair, her heart was far from being at rest ; it remained a prey to torturing fears, and at times the longing for some sign or word reassuring her about her husband's fate, amounted to agony. She continued, meanwhile, to seek comfort in prayer, and was faithful to her habit of performing the Stations of the Cross daily.

'Perhaps God will have foreseen my tears and supplications, and answered them beforehand,' she would say, in moments when the sense of His mercy was lively and present; but the doubts would return, and plunge her once more into anguish.

Aline felt deeply for her friend, and did all that faith and sympathy could suggest to console her at such times, and to raise and strengthen her hopes in the divine goodness. One day, seeing her more depressed than usual, she said, 'Why should you not go and see the Curé d'Ars? He has a wonderful power of consolation, they say, as well as a gift of prophecy. If you like, I will go with you.'

Madame X—— was overjoyed at the proposal, and the two set off together. Aline had long wished to see the saintly old man, the fame of whose miraculous gifts was drawing pilgrims from all parts of the world to his confessional; she was anxious to have his advice on a point which had been causing her great perplexity, and which she fancied her confessor did not fully understand.

On arriving at Ars, the travellers found the little church crowded to overflowing, and they were told that numbers had been waiting three days and nights for their turn to enter the confessional. Aline and her friend looked at one another in dismay. The spirit was indeed willing, but the flesh was weak, and it would have been a matter of simple impossibility for either of them to perform a similar feat of patience. In their despair, they went to consult with the sacristan. M. le Curé had just left the church for his frugal midday meal of herbs and bread and water, and was to return when it was over. Could not the sacristan let them in by a side door where they might waylay the holy man on his way back? This was, however, it seemed, strictly forbidden. Almost everybody who came had some reason to show why he or she should be attended to before anybody else, and, except in case of illness, no one was allowed to break through the lines.

'But I will tell you what to do, mesdames,' said the sacristan; 'stand up somewhere within sight, and if it is really needful for your souls to speak to M. le Curé, and that you cannot wait, the good God will point you out to him, and he will call you up at once.'

Following this advice, they elbowed their way through the crowd, and took their stand as near the front as possible, and waited until the sacristy door opened, and M. le Curé's venerable white head appeared. He stood for a moment surveying the crowd of eager reverent faces with his mild, child-like gaze, and then, fixing it on Madame X——, beckoned her to approach. The crowd made way at once, and she advanced, her heart beating violently as she knelt down to receive his blessing and begin her confession. Before, however, she had opened her lips, the Curé whispered:

'You have no need to confess, my child; you have not come for direction, but for consolation. Be comforted! Your husband has found mercy. Your Stations of the Cross have saved him. Continue to pray for the repose of his soul.' He blessed her, and she withdrew without having spoken a single word. He then beckoned to Aline.

'*Mon père*,' she began, 'I wish to make a general confession to you.'.

'It is not necessary, my child; your confessor has all the light that is essential for your guidance. Continue to do so and so—' And the servant of

God added a few words of advice, which proved that he had the clearest insight into the state of her soul. The two friends made their act of thanksgiving, and left Ars the same day.

About a year after this incident, Aline's health became so much worse that her family insisted on having fresh advice. Accordingly, she came to Paris, and Dr. J——, the then highest authority in cases of the kind, was called in. The old story of neuralgia, nerves, and so forth, which had been the refrain of all former medical men, was now pronounced a gross delusion, and the case declared one of organic disease, far, if not indeed fatally, advanced. Before, however, undertaking the case, Dr. J—— sought a consultation with four other eminent physicians. All four agreed that the malady was incurable. One was of opinion that the patient had three months to live; the others gave her six, or nine at a stretch. Dr. J—— alone declared that he would prolong her life four years at the least, while he was not without a hope of saving her life altogether, and effecting a complete cure.

These various opinions were submitted to Aline, and she heard them with as much *sang-froid* as if it had been a question of spending the winter in Paris or in the country, discussed the *pros* and *cons* of each in a business-like manner, and ended by adopting Dr. J——'s verdict, and placing herself unreservedly in his hands.

The extraordinary coolness which she showed in the whole matter was, no doubt, characteristic; but on the other hand she was upheld by the conviction that, come what might, let her be ever so incurably ill, she could not die until her children were educated, and one of them, at least, settled in life. This was the mainspring of the confidence which she yielded so fully and spontaneously to Dr. J——'s promise. Madame André was but too willing to believe and to hope; but in spite of herself, her heart sank in proportion as Aline's sanguine hopes took the old dreaded form of conviction; she felt, as before, a prophetic fear that it would end in disappointment.

'I don't feel at all sure of being cured, mother,' Aline would say; 'but I am perfectly certain that I shall live until my work is done; as certain as I am of my existence. Probably I shall have a terrible time of it; but what does that signify? If only our dear Lord would give me the use of my legs! *Une mère de famille sans jambes, vous avouerez que cela n'a pas le sens commun!*'

In the next breath she would express her perfect readiness to be a cripple to the end, if it so pleased Almighty God; but never, even in passing, did she speak of her death as a probability to be contemplated. With this one exception, the will of God may be said to have been her daily bread. Her first desire in every undertaking, great and small, in every pain, in every proposed alleviation, in every act of her life, was to ascertain what was most pleasing to that divine will, and to accomplish it at every and any cost.

From the moment she placed herself in the hands of Dr. J——, her life became one of poignant privation. She may be said to have been bedridden; for with the exception of occasionally rising for a few hours in the afternoon, she never left her bed but to have it made. This forced inactivity was, in itself, an acute suffering to one whose ardent nature and buoyant temperament made exercise and constant occupation as necessary to her as air is to others. But she bore it as brightly as if it had been a matter of choice, and the most agreeable kind of life to her. Her room was the rendezvous of a little circle of friends who found delight in her society, and who carried away from it more brightness than they could contribute with all their anecdotes, and the fresh news that each was eager to

L

bring to the sick-room from the busy world outside. The loss of her daily Mass, and all the soul-stirring functions of the Church in which Aline ever found such consolation, was one of the heaviest of her trials ; but it was borne like the rest, uncomplainingly. She was subjected, periodically, to operations of the most painful nature, but these were red-letter days to the sufferer. It was not merely that she was resigned to suffering ; she seemed to joy in it. I remember how we all laughed one day when the Sœur de Bon Secours who was attending her, exclaimed almost snappishly, *apropos* of Aline's expressing some surprise at a person who had been rather cowardly under an operation performed the day before by Dr. J——:

'O, it is easy for you to talk, madame, you who jump at suffering as a cat jumps at milk !'

I can see Aline now, sitting propped up against her pillows, and laughing louder than any of us at the Sister's simile and the vehement way she expressed it.

Brave, gentle sufferer ! Many a laugh she gave us from her bed of pain. We used to twit her with being so coquettish in the said bed—most Frenchwomen have this weakness—and certainly the bank of snowy pillows, befrilled and embroidered, the dainty cap, the soft draperies of lace and cambric that composed her costume, made a wonderfully becoming *mise en scène*, and set off her alabaster complexion and sloe-black eyes to great advantage. She was not at all handsome; her features were quite irregular, and yet, somehow, they produced the effect of beauty. There was a mobility, a piquancy, and a charm of expression in her face that no one could resist; her forehead was as smooth and white as marble, and her eyes the most expressive I ever saw in a human head; fiery and tender, flashing and melting as each changing emotion stirred her soul.

Madame André used to say she defied any one to inflict a pang of self-love on Aline, because self-love was dead in her. Of course this must have been an exaggeration, since we have the word of a saint for it that self-love only dies a quarter of an hour before self. But Aline certainly had the familiar demon under such good control that those who knew her best and watched her most closely, failed to detect its presence. She was, perhaps, as free from human respect as any one short of a saint can be. By nature she was inclined to a certain fastidious elegance in her dress, and her husband, like a true Frenchman, fostered this inclination, and liked to see her beautifully attired at all times; but, early of a morning, she used to steal a march on him, and run out to Mass so shabbily dressed that you would have taken her for a poor woman going off to her day's work. She carried this eccentricity so far, at last, that her mother remonstrated with her. Aline blushed, and replied laughingly:

'*Ma mère*, it is only a poor little pretence at practising poverty. Don't grudge me the pleasure; it hurts nobody.'

At the end of two years of a life such as I have described, Aline so far vindicated Dr. J——'s opposition to his colleagues that she was able to resume something like an ordinary manner of life. She now rose every day, and was able to walk short distances. I shall never forget the first time she went out for a walk with her three children. Some few friends had assembled to see her go forth, and make a little *festa* of the event. The mother's face literally shone with happiness as we wished her good speed.

The following winter was one of comparative health to Aline. She was still carried up and down stairs; but with this exception, she was able to live pretty much like other people. Her gratitude for this partial restoration poured itself forth in many channels. Masses were said for the souls in Purgatory, abundant alms flowed into the homes of the poor, fresh orphans were adopted, and novenas made at the numerous shrines where prayers had been offered up for her recovery. She placed, as a votive offering, in the church of Notre Dame des Victoires, a marble slab, bearing the inscription: ' J'ai invoqué Marie, et elle m'a exaucée ; que son nom soit béni !'

Would that I could prolong this happy period! But it was only a palm-tree by the wayside, a well in the wilderness, where the pilgrim was allowed to drink and 'rest a little while' before resuming her journey along the thorny path that remained yet to be traversed.

She was going on as usual, when one morning, quite suddenly, she was seized with a pain in the shoulder, accompanied by a swelling. It increased so rapidly in violence, that those about her concluded it was either an acute attack of rheumatism, or that she sprained herself in the night without noticing it. Aline inclined to the latter idea, and yielded to her mother's advice that they should send for a woman, who was very skilful in that line, to rub the part. This operation was repeated for a couple of days, and then the lump became suddenly much larger, and the pain increased until the agony was too much for even Aline's courage, and she cried and groaned aloud. I cannot even now think, without a shudder, of the torture thus ignorantly inflicted on the poor little frame that had such cruel sufferings yet in store for it.

Madame André wrote to my mother at the end of nearly a week, and begged her to go and inform Dr. J—— of what had happened, and consult him as to what should be done. When he heard the story, he bounded in his chair, and struck the table with his clenched hand.

'Good heavens!' he cried, 'telegraph to them to bring her up by the first train that starts. God grant it be not too late!'

There was no time to look for lodgings. We telegraphed for Madame André and Aline to come straight to our house. They arrived late that night. Aline was suffering intensely, and was put to bed at once. Soon after daybreak next morning Dr. J—— came up to see her. The moment he laid his hand on the inflamed shoulder, indeed before he had seen it at all, his opinion was formed.

'This must be opened at once,' he said, speaking very coolly (a sinister sign to those who knew his moods); 'I will come at eleven to-morrow morning to perform the operation.'

'Will you give me chloroform?' inquired Aline.

'Do you wish it?'

'No.'

'No more do I.'

And nothing more was said about it. Dr. J—— left the room to give the necessary directions. A stretcher was to be provided for the patient to lie on during the operation; some other preparations were to be made, and Aline was to be kept as quiet as possible. This was no easy matter, for everything had to be got ready under her eyes; the effect was, however, not to frighten or depress, but rather to elate her dangerously. She was in a state of high excitement the whole day, talking with animation to every one who came in, joking about the event of the morrow as if it were something quite comical, even enjoyable on the whole. In one sense it was enjoyable. The prospect of a good sharp suffering always had an exhilarating effect on her ardent soul; and the gracious, nay, the exulting way in which she welcomed the cross, amply justified the Sister's remark, that the cat did not take to its favourite food more lovingly than Aline did to pain.

Poor Madame André was less heroic, and while

she moved about, seeing to the few necessary preliminaries, one would have imagined it was she who had to undergo the operation rather than her daughter. She was as white as a ghost, too weak almost to stand, yet too agitated to sit still. I can see her walking from room to room with clasped hands, now muttering prayers for courage, now bursting out into bitter lamentations over the cruel destiny that condemned her to stand, like the Mother of Sorrows, by the cross, while her child was given up to the torturers. She strove hard to keep up an appearance of calm before Aline; but the latter knew her too well to be deceived, and the effort to impart to her mother some of the divine strength that she enjoyed herself was not the lightest part of her burden.

We went off, we three at home, to get a Mass at Notre Dame des Victoires for the morrow, and to bespeak as many prayers as we could amongst our friends. The Abbé V——, Aline's confessor, came to see her early in the morning, after having offered the Holy Sacrifice for her, and then everything was ready.

Punctually at the appointed hour the dreaded ring was heard at the door, and the four medical men were ushered in. My mother had gone to the neighbouring church to spend the interval before the Blessed Sacrament; my sister and I remained in the next room with Madame André saying the litanies. We guessed pretty nearly when the operation began, but not a sound came from the patient; we heard nothing but the voice of the operating surgeon, speaking in angry tones, sending his colleagues to the right-abouts, scolding the Sœur de Bon Secours, the maid, everybody in turns; this was his custom, adopted partly with a view to distract the patient from her suffering, partly as a mask for his own emotion.

My mother returned just as all was over. We were standing in the ante-chamber when the medical men came out; none of them spoke, except Dr. J——, who stopped and talked in his usual loud tones, cheerfully enough, if we might have trusted to that. He was strong in his praise of his *vaillante petite malade*, and said the operation had gone off splendidly. He then hurried away, with a parting injunction to keep the sick-room as quiet as possible; we might go in one by one to look at the patient for a moment; but no one was to speak to her. Madame André, of course, went first. She came out after a moment, holding up her hands in amazement. 'Will you believe it! She actually made a face at me! I really think she has not suffered anything to speak of,' was her exclamation. My mother, greatly relieved, but still nervous, and with traces of recent tears on her face, went in next, treading softly, for the doctor had said that the slightest vibration would affect the sensitive wound. She stole a timid glance at the bed. Aline had one hand free, the left; she drew it slowly from under the clothes, and put her finger to her nose with such an irresistibly droll expression that my mother, in spite of herself, was obliged to laugh.

Was it, then, true, that she had not suffered? She had suffered to the point of agony. The surgeon had been obliged to cut very deep into the flesh, quite to the bone, and then.... One of the assistants, meantime, knelt beside the stretcher; Aline grasped his shoulder with one hand, while the other held the crucifix; she thrust her head into his breast to keep herself steady; and such preternatural strength did the violence of the pain lend her, that although he was a stout broad-shouldered man, and she a small fragile little creature, he declared it was all he could do not to fall backwards. She had a lawn handkerchief folded in many doubles between her teeth, and when the operation was over she had bitten it through. She told us herself that for about two minutes the agony was so terrific that it seemed to lift her off the bed: she could not conceive herself living through it one minute longer. Yet when I said what a pity it was that she had not taken chloroform and thus escaped the fiercest part of the suffering, she answered with a look in her eyes that I shall never forget, ' Ah, *ma chère*, but what a pity it would have been to lose it! I offered it up for the conversion of E——. Only think if it obtains that!'

Of course it was out of the question now, her being moved to an hotel; we, therefore, had the consolation of keeping her with us, and doing what friendship might do to alleviate her sufferings during those terrible days. They were very precious days to me. The hours that I spent with her alone, conversing on those subjects always nearest her heart, God, His dealings with souls, the mystery of life in its ever-varying phases, were a source of inexhaustible edification and delight to me.

The 'exaltation' which had so miraculously, as I may call it, sustained the sufferer on the day of the operation, passed away when its work was done; but it was not followed, as is so often the case, by any reaction of despondency or physical depression.

She retained all her playful gaiety of manner, and those who saw her through that trying period would agree with me that it was she who cheered and supported us, rather than we her. Many a time we have stood round her bed while the wound was being dressed, and been obliged to suspend the operation from the fits of laughing she would send us into by one of her droll *sorties*, the Sister starting back with the sponge, or some other appliance in her hand, so as not to touch the wound, while herself and the patient shook with laughter ; and when sometimes, with all her care, the nurse could not avoid inflicting a twinge of pain, Aline would make some grotesque noise, imitating an animal, or something of that sort, so as to leave the Sister, who could not see her face, in doubt whether it was fun, or pain that made her cry out.

But she had only now arrived at the first step of the Calvary that was yet to be climbed. In about three weeks another tumour, which had rapidly formed on the right side, had to be opened. Aline heard the announcement of the second operation with perfect coolness, and if she did not evince the same kind of radiant satisfaction as in the case of the first, she was ready to meet it with a serenity of fortitude that was the more remarkable, considering how much her mental and bodily strength had been drawn upon since then. But Madame André almost broke down under this second trial. She came in, clasping her hands, and looking the very picture of despair. Aline burst out laughing.

'Eh, what will you, *ma mère!*' she exclaimed. 'I am well served! I have always asked to have my purgatory in this world, so that I may walk straight into heaven when I die, and our good God is taking me at my word. Then you know I have always declared that I should have a *place réservée* in heaven, up by St. Teresa and St. Augustine; serve me right again! When people have such pretensions they must expect to pay for them!'

What could Madame André say? Nothing, except that God was, indeed, taking her at her word. We were now very anxious that she should have chloroform; it seemed impossible that the frail exhausted little body could undergo the fresh ordeal without the merciful help of that boon of modern science. But Aline would not hear of it. It was very well for children and pagans to have recourse to such things; but grown-up Christians ought to know better than to cheat themselves out of their inheritance in that fashion. What was the use of operations or suffering at all if they could not be turned into merit, if they could not show our dear Lord we could endure something for His sake? We, poor cowards, had no arguments against such logic as this; so the operation was performed as before, with the superadded horror of experience to intensify the pain.

From this time forth Aline's life was a prolonged martyrdom. The dressing of the wounds morning and evening was positive torture, while the position of the tumours, one high up on the left shoulder, the other in front on the right side, made it impossible for the body to rest its weight anywhere. This was, perhaps, the most acute of her sufferings; the constant strain, the effort to prevent her weight pressing on the wounded parts, was worse than actual pain. Cushions of every shape and size were made, in order to isolate the wounds from contact and pressure, as far as it was possible, but the result was little more than a momentary alleviation.

I remember one morning when I went in to inquire how she had spent the night, she said: '*Ma petite*, I have realised one of the pains of the damned: complete immobility in bodily torture. I was very cowardly; I could not help crying, do you know, and asking our Lord to give me just one quarter of an hour's respite!' The tears gathered as she spoke; but she added quickly, with one of her old smiles: 'It *was* very cowardly! He did not ask for a minute's respite on the Cross.'

A period of spiritual desolation was now approaching, during which Aline was called upon to endure the most awful of all interior trials, the one which wrung from the Man-God in His agony that cry of sorrow and reproach: 'My God, My God, why hast Thou forsaken Me!' She felt herself forsaken. The unction and the light which had hitherto made the cross easy and robbed the chalice of its bitterness were withdrawn, and she was left to toil on under the burden, alone and in the darkness. Alone? She thought so, or else where would have been the trial? But we know that God is never so near a soul as when He thus hides Himself, trusting her love to follow Him out into the night and watch with Him in the starless gloom of Olivet.

It was not the dread of death that quenched the light to Aline, and made her courage quail; it was the dread of leaving her children, of leaving them without a guide who would care for their souls, and look to the one thing necessary. Their natural guardian would be an uncle, who, if he believed they had such possessions as souls at all, would be sure to trouble himself very little about them. Any Christian mother might tremble at the thought of abandoning her children to such guardianship; the prospect was so intolerable to Aline that she turned from it in absolute despair. Her faith, generous and full of trust as it was, could not reach to such an act of abandonment as this. She could not reconcile it with the mercy, or even the justice, of Almighty God, that He should ask it of her; yet the idea that she was rapidly approaching the end was now almost a conviction. She told me—not at the time, but when the trial was past—that she seemed to see Death always before her, standing behind a door that stood open from her bedroom into the drawing-room; he was like a fixture there, a skeleton, grinning at her with a scythe in his hand; no matter who came in, or how full the room was, there stood the ghastly watcher, with his sightless eyes staring at her from behind the door; at night, when she lay awake in the dark, she saw him as distinctly as in broad daylight. She began to think, at last, that she beheld it with her corporal eyes, and that the delusion was a sign of approaching madness. No person about her had the least suspicion of what she was enduring. She complained to no one but God.

Madame André, meantime, shared these fears, though in a different way. Dr. J——, from the day of the last operation, had said nothing that betrayed his opinion one way or the other; but he was extremely quiet in his manner, and civil to everybody—a fact which, as I said, boded no good. When he was satisfied with the way a case was going on, he came and went like a tempest, slamming the doors, shouting at the top of his voice as if everybody were stone deaf, and demeaning himself generally in a tempestuous manner. It was, therefore, with growing uneasiness that day by day we noticed him subsiding into civility and gentleness. This, however, did not last long; perhaps a fortnight or so, and then, to the immense relief of us all, the storm began to growl, the doctor stamped and swore, and returned to his normal state of boisterous violence. He would burst into Aline's room of a morning, and begin to bully everybody and make noise enough to bring the house down. The patient's spirits rose quickly under the influence of this beneficent change, and she gradually regained her old serenity and cheerfulness.

All this time the children were in the country under the care of near relations, and a staff of trusty old servants; but if they had been alone on a desert island their mother could scarcely have been in greater anxiety about them. They took it in turn to write every day for some weeks, and nothing could be more completely reassuring than the tone of this correspondence ; but one morning Madame André received a letter announcing that the two elder girls had caught the measles. It would have been impossible to keep the accident a secret from Aline ; but who was to break it to her? Her mother, after much hesitation, and with the tenderest precautions, told her the truth. She was like one distraught. It was a judgment on her. Why had she forsaken her children to look after her own health?

Her confessor was sent for, and his influence, after a while, brought her round to a more reasonable state of mind. The weeks that followed were nevertheless a period of indescribable misery to her, although the daily bulletins were as satisfactory as could be. The third child caught the malady in due course ; but all three had it in a very mild form, and were convalescent within the shortest time possible. As soon as it was safe to contemplate the journey, Aline insisted they should come to Paris. She would take an apartment, and be carried there beforehand to receive them on their arrival. There was a general outcry at this. Dr

J—— was furious; Madame André was terrified; everybody entreated and remonstrated; but we might as well have been talking to the man in the moon. Aline had made up her mind; at all risks to herself she should have her children with her.

'You believe really, then,' I could not help saying to her, 'that Almighty God cannot take care of them without you, and that if you had been there they would not have caught the measles?'

'*Ma petite*,' she said—I was a head taller than she, but being a good deal younger, she always called me *ma petite*—' a mother is the visible representative of Providence on earth; it is my duty to be near my children, and if I forsake my duty I am answerable for what may come of it.'

A large apartment was taken in the Champs Elysées, and the thing now to be considered was how Aline was to get there. Her own idea was to be carried on a hospital stretcher, as the poor people are. Perhaps the resemblance was one of the attractions for this mode of conveyance; but Dr. J——, who had no such predilection in his mind, at once ridiculed and dismissed the plan. It was decided finally that she should be rolled up in her blankets, and placed in a carriage, every precaution being taken against her catching cold, which, far more than the pain of the transit, was what the doctor dreaded.

The journey, which lasted about a quarter of an hour from door to door, was effected without inconvenience or accident, and the presence of her children had such a beneficial effect on the patient as to fully justify her maternal instinct in risking everything to be with them. The sound of their voices revived her, she declared, like fresh air, and even the din of the practising, which, needless to say, went on as energetically as ever, seemed to have a soothing effect on her nerves.

Things went on without any sensible alteration until the summer had set in, and then the whole party went to the seaside.

They returned with the invalid pretty much the same as when she left. The change had produced some general improvement; she ate and slept better; but the march continued to be steadily downwards; she was thin to emaciation, and pale to ghastliness; the flow from the two wounds was as copious as in the first days, and was slowly, but steadily draining away her life. Dr. J—— was gradually relapsing into a disquieting gentleness. He spoke reassuringly, but no one was deceived by this; no one but the patient herself, who, in proportion as hope died away from every one around her, grew sanguine. She had, in fact, worked back to the old conviction that her death was impossible, that it was only a question of time, and of more or less suffering until her health was restored.

'I know,' she would say sometimes, 'that it is extremely doubtful whether I shall ever make what you call a recovery of it; it is quite possible—in fact I think it is very likely—that I shall be a kind of invalid all my life; but I find that in reality that does not so much matter; I see that I can superintend the education of the children as effectively as if I had the use of my legs and were always in the midst of them; so I am quite ready to be a cripple to the end of my days if our Lord so wills it.'

The Sœur de Bon Secours would venture, perhaps, to hint at the desirableness of being ready to make even the sacrifice of her life if our Lord so willed it; but Aline would smile, and say something about that being a very natural thought for a religious, but that a mother had more insight to God's will when her children were concerned. How could it be His will to send three immortal souls adrift in life with no protector? For Madame André did not count; she was in wretched health and not likely to survive the shock of Aline's death many months, and then the children would be at the mercy of their uncle, who would marry them off as fast as he could to three eligible young men, never troubling himself whether they were Turks, Jews, or Atheists, provided they were otherwise qualified to make good husbands. Madame André and the Abbé V—— looked on and listened with the deepest anxiety while Aline expressed herself in this strain.

'It is very sad, but let it not disquiet us,' said the Abbé one morning on leaving the sick-room: 'God will dispel the delusion in good time; you will see, He never will allow so generous a soul to die in such dispositions.'

He did not, at the same time, disguise from Madame André that it made him anxious, and he left nothing undone himself to open the eyes of his penitent to the peril of clinging so obstinately to her own will. The error was all the more dangerous from the fact of its being rooted in Aline's indomitable faith. I have known many persons of strong and ardent faith, but I never knew any whose faith resembled hers; there was something of her own peculiar originality about it. If it did not sound profane, I would say that there was an element of humour in it. She would argue the point with our Lord, like the woman of Canaan, bringing up His own words to Him with a boldness that would have come near irreverence on the lips of one who loved less, and whose soul was less controlled by that humble fear on which true love is built. But with her it was a child arguing with a fond, tender father, who *might* be coaxed into yielding, though it was possible he would remain inexorable. There was opposite her bed a touching picture of our Saviour carrying the Cross; Aline's eyes were constantly seeking this picture, dwelling on it with a long look of mingled compassion, entreaty, and reproach that were more touching and expressive than any words. She seemed to be holding a conversation with the thorn-crowned Head, listening and answering in silence; then suddenly she would make a speaking-trumpet of her hand and shout out to it, startling us all:

'*Mon bon Jésus!* I don't speak loud enough that is why You don't answer me! Well, now I am going to shout at the very top of my voice, so that You *must* hear me!' Then she would turn on us, and say that we, too, prayed in whispers, *du bout des lèvres*, and this was why our prayers were not heard. 'You should "shout out" like the prophet,' she would say, 'and then they would hear you, *là haut*, and give you what you want just to get rid of you. You know what our Lord says Himself about importuning Him, and hammering at the door until it is opened!'

God was a living presence to Aline. We would all say, no doubt, that He is a living presence to us. But practically He is not. He is an Almighty power dwelling in some region beyond and above us, an omnipotent abstract Being to be invoked; a Law, a Fear, a Religion, anything and everything short of a close living presence, a Person here in the room with us—with me as I write, with you as you read—seeing, hearing, touching us. God was really this to Aline. And so with our Lady and the saints and angels. They were living personal friends, invisible, but present and close; persons whom she could speak to, and who were listening to her as we were.

'Dear Mother!' she would cry, closing her poor little wasted hand, and speaking through it in a loud whisper, 'are you deaf, or are you angry? Why don't you answer me! It's not kind. Ask your dear little Jesus to do what I want; coax Him for this next feast! You *know* He won't refuse you!'

But the one thing she thus persistently implored was the one that was persistently denied. She was wasting away so visibly that, to all who saw her, life was now a question not of years, scarcely even of months. For it was difficult to believe that nature could hold out much longer. The process of dressing the wounds was daily becoming one of greater torture. The body was so sensitive that it was impossible to lay a finger even on the sound parts without causing her exquisite pain; all the contrivances which had hitherto afforded some relief had become useless; we were obliged to turn her in the bed with sheets folded like swathing bands; the effort of lifting her to a sitting posture for the purpose of dressing the shoulder was performed with the utmost difficulty: her maid bent over her on the bed, Aline clasped both hands round the woman's neck, and was slowly lifted up as the latter rose. Those hands, once so beautiful, were now so distorted as to resemble claws rather than human hands, and so sensitive that to support herself while sitting up, she was obliged to clutch the end of an eiderdown pillow; she dared not hold by any one, lest an involuntary pressure should hurt the fingers and send the pain tingling all over her body. As long as it was possible, the doctor insisted on her being taken up every day for a couple of hours, and carried into the drawing-room for change of air. But as spring came on, this had to be given up; the only alleviation henceforth possible was obtained by constantly changing the pillows and little cushions, so as to cool the feverish and emaciated body. The Sisters in attendance—there were two now, one for the day and one for the night—declared they had never seen anything living so thin; the frame was exactly like a skeleton, the mere wreck of a body. Yet even in this extremity Aline retained her old brightness to an extraordinary degree. Her sickroom was still the rendezvous of a circle of friends who seldom let a day pass without coming to see her. She took the liveliest interest in everything that was going on in the world outside. The elections were taking place just then, and she followed the struggle between the various candidates with an excitement that was surprising to us all. Every new book that appeared on a sympathetic subject was an event of interest to her; she was not able to read, or even to be read to, except for a few minutes at a time, and then she reserved her strength for some spiritual work; but she liked us to read other books, and then to tell her about them. I happened to be reading *Frank Fairleigh* at the time, and I always feel grateful to the author of that charming novel when I recall the delight it afforded my friend. I can see her now laughing heartily over the hero's comical adventures, and exclaiming when I had finished retailing my narrative for the day, 'Ah, *ma petite*, why have we not the sense to write books like that in French! Clever and spirited, and yet so innocent that while old people can enjoy them, the young may read them with impunity.'

But a day came at last, when Aline was compelled to acknowledge that the sacrifice which she had considered impossible, and recoiled from so obstinately, was, in truth, demanded of her.

I might be tempted to conceal, or at least to be partly silent as to the effect of this conviction on my friend, if I were not adhering rigorously to facts, and describing them, not as I might have wished them to be, but as they really were.

When she first awoke to the reality of her state, and came face to face with the certainty that her recovery, admitting that it was yet possible, was altogether improbable, her first impulse was to bow unmurmuringly to the will of God. But beneath this act of conformity there lurked in some secret fold of her heart the hope, almost the belief, that the sacrifice was still a good way off, and might, by dint of prayer, be postponed still further. At least, looking at things in the light of subsequent events, this is how it strikes one. Madame André was less serene in her resignation. If her faith never failed, there were moments when the sight of her child's sufferings tried it to its foundations, and when the *fiat* of submission, so bravely uttered by the victim, seemed beyond the mother's strength.

At such times Aline was the one who strove to encourage and uphold her. '*Ma pauvre mère !*' she would say, shaking her head with an affectionate smile, 'how *can* you doubt but that it is good and best for me to be as I am? You know I am here by God's will, and so long as we are sure of that what does the rest matter? What does the time, or the manner, or anything else signify?'

But while Madame André agreed with the principle of this, the application of it was more than she could bear. It was the doctors' doing in a great measure, she argued ; they had misunderstood and mismanaged the case so long! If they had not been so ignorant, how much of this torture might have been avoided! It was easy to bow to God's will, but the stupidity of human beings was not so easy to forgive. Poor dear Madame André!

She was like the rest of us. It was the old story of Balaam beating his ass because he himself could not see the angel that was stopping the way.

The removal of the broken splinters of bone from the wounds necessitated most painful operations from time to time, and these afforded Aline rich opportunities for the exercise of fortitude and suffering love. She continued her practice of offering up the pain on each occasion, first for the soul of her husband, and then for the conversion of some sinner, and the relief of the souls in purgatory. Finally, however, one day on coming out of her room after one of these operations, Dr. J—— declared that it should be the last; he would inflict no more useless torture on her. It may be that the agitation of his countenance, or some expression that escaped him in the room, informed Aline of this determination, but from that day forth a change came over her. She never alluded again to her recovery, but fell into a state of complete dejection. It was evident to those around her that she had relinquished all hope of life; it was equally clear to the few who could read the silent symptoms of her soul that she recoiled more than ever from the thought of death. She could not accept it. She could not bring her mind to see how it could be God's will, or to reconcile the decree with His mercy, nay, with His justice. I recall even now with pain the effect some words of hers produced on me at the time, and I think it was the same day that the Abbé V—— came out of her room with a look of distress on his kind face that he did not attempt to conceal.

'Pray, pray with all your hearts!' he said; 'it is awful to see her in this state. But God is merciful; He will open her eyes; it cannot last so to the end!'

Meantime, the blindness was terrible to those who only saw the present, and could not see beyond. Things were at this point when one afternoon, early in the month of May, two Sisters of Charity came to pay Aline a visit. They were full of a miracle which had taken place a few days previously in the church of the Lazarists, where the relics of St. Vincent de Paul were exposed; I do not remember whether there was any fête of the Order just then, or whether it was simply because of the month of May; but the miracle was a striking one. A young girl, who had for years been completely paralysed, made a novena to our Lady and St. Vincent, and was carried into the church on the ninth day, heard Mass there, and immediately after rose up and walked out of the church perfectly cured. One of the Sisters who related the event had been an eye-

witness of it. They entreated Aline to make a
novena to their saintly founder, and go to venerate
his relics on the closing day, promising that the
entire community would join with her in it. She
took fire at once. It was arranged there and then
that she should begin the novena next day, letters
being despatched to other friends and communities
inviting them to join in it. I came in, soon after the
Sisters' departure, and found her in the highest state
of excitement. She was going to be miraculously
cured! There was no other way for it. The doctors had brought her to death's door, and could do
nothing now but bury her. Well, our good God
was going to let them see! He would speak the
word, and their proud science should be confounded;
they would see her made whole by faith, by the sole
power of God, when all human remedies had failed.
She continued in this state of elation all day. Every
person who came in was requisitioned to join in the
novena; the miracle was announced as if it were
already performed.

'Only fancy the astonishment of *le papa* J——,'
as she called the doctor, 'when he comes in and
sees me up and dressed and advancing to receive
him! What a triumph it will be to show him how
the *bon Dieu* can *planter* the learned faculty, and

send their fine science to the rightabouts! If it only converts him! He is sound at heart, *le papa* J——; I have great hopes that it will.'

A few days later, when the prayers were going on in every direction, the Baronne de R——, a friend of Madame André's, came in to say goodbye; she was leaving Paris, and expressed her regret at having to go before the novena was out.

'Yes, I am sorry you will not be here to witness the miracle,' said Aline, 'but I will telegraph to you on my way home from the church, so that you may say the *Te Deum* for me at once.'

Madame André listened, and groaned in spirit. She had so often seen Aline *exaltée* in this way. She remembered how it had been before her husband's death, how buoyed up she had been with hopes of a miraculous cure, and how those hopes had been deceived. She forbore from a word that could betray how little she shared the present anticipations; but Aline, who read her mother's face like an open book, remonstrated with her in her own fashion. '*Ma mère*, it is clearer than ever to me at this moment that I cannot die, and yet die I must without a miracle; God knows that, and He is going to perform the miracle. Patience! a few days longer and you will see!'

An incident occurred during the novena which deeply distressed Aline. The Abbé V——, who was, of course, joining in the prayers, though imploring a different miracle, came one morning to give her Holy Communion; owing to some unforeseen circumstance, he came earlier than his wont, and none of the servants were down; so after ringing several times, and waiting nearly a quarter of an hour, he was obliged to go away. When he told Aline of this next day, her grief was inconsolable; she burst into tears, and sobbed as if her heart would break. 'O, to think of His coming and knocking and waiting at the door, and having to go away!' she cried, kissing her little crucifix again and again; 'O, *mon pauvre Jésus!* I did not mean it! I never heard You!' It was all the Abbé V—— could do to console her, and when some hours later I came in, her eyes were still red, and her first words were to tell me of the *malheur* that had happened her the day before.

It had been a serious preoccupation from the first, how Aline was to get to the church. Her going in a carriage was now out of the question; she could not have borne the jolting even at a foot pace, and on a stretcher she would have been too much exposed to take cold. The only possible conveyance we could think of was a sedan-chair. It was settled, therefore, that she should go in one.

But, as we soon discovered, this was easier said than done. We scoured Paris in vain for a specimen of that antique conveyance so dear to our great-grandmothers. At last some one had the bright idea of writing to the director of the opera, and asking for the loan of one. I do not think the precise motive of the proposed journey was explained, but anyhow, the director sent a most courteous reply, informing Madame André that the largest and handsomest *chaise-à-porteurs* in the *garde-meuble* of the opera was at her disposal, and would be at her door punctually on the morning she named.

And so it was. Good gracious, shall I ever forget it! We were in the *salon* when it arrived; the doors were thrown open, and in tramped two porters of seemingly gigantic stature, carrying between them a gorgeous machine all gold without and crimson within, with a royal crown on top of it, gilt cupids perched on the corners, royal arms emblazoned on the panels, neither more nor less, in fact, than the chair used by Catherine de' Medicis in the opera of the *Huguenots*. A cry of dismay greeted the apparition, and we rushed in to tell Aline. Of course the pilgrimage was at an end; the idea of making an exhibition of herself in the streets in this harlequin's coach was not to be thought of. But Aline was delighted.

'The very thing!' she cried, when it was brought in for her inspection; 'they will take us for a masquerade, and so we are! Just look! Did any one ever see such a figure off the stage, or out of the churchyard!' And she held up her poor skeleton hands and laughed at them. Brave, gentle martyr! Weary were the days and nights that had brought her to this figure that she was so ready to laugh at.

There was no question of dressing her. She was rolled up in an immense cloak of the flimsiest sarcenet, lined with quilted eiderdown, which had been made on purpose for the occasion, so as to combine both warmth and lightness as much as possible. One of the big porters caught her up as if she had been a bundle. We could hardly repress a scream as we saw him whip her up so unceremoniously, and, without more ado, squeeze her in through the narrow door; but he evidently did not hurt her the least bit, for she was laughing all the time. It was like a beginning of the miracle, for the nurses could scarcely touch her with their tender skilful fingers without making her wince. Just as she was packed up, and every one was ready, a loud ring at the door caused a frightful panic. If it should be Dr. J——!

'*Ces messieurs,*' said Aline, pointing to the burly porters, 'will have the kindness to throw me out of the window, and you will all jump after me. There is nothing else for it!'

Happily it turned out to be a false alarm; and after we had all drawn a breath of relief, the *cortège*, the strangest, assuredly, ever witnessed by the streets of Paris, so used to strange spectacles, sallied forth on its way. I remained behind, ostensibly that some one might be there to welcome Aline on her return. The truth was I had not the courage to go with them. Madame André went in the carriage with the youngest girl; the other two walked on one side of the chair, and a Sœur de Bon Secours on the other. The crimson blinds were drawn down; but Aline could peep through them, and got more than one fright, fancying that she saw the doctor's familiar chocolate-coloured *coupé* coming upon them.

I stood at the drawing-room window and watched the little caravan until it was out of sight. Then I knelt down and joined in the litanies and psalms which the pilgrims were to recite on the way. It was a miserable dreary morning, more like March than

May; the sky was leaden colour; it had rained in the night, and a drizzly rain was falling still; everything was calculated to damp one's spirit. Aline had first announced her intention of walking home, and it was only when the effect she would produce on the *trottoir*, in her floating mantle of eiderdown, was made apparent to her, that she reluctantly consented to abandon this triumphal march, and to drive back in the carriage with her mother. The distance from the Champs Elysées to the Rue de Sèvres, going at the pace they were obliged to keep, was calculated to take about an hour, and the same back; so, allowing half an hour to remain in the church, they could not be home before half-past one.

Several friends came in to await the return of the expedition. I was too excited to talk, so I went into Madame André's room, which was off the *salon*, opposite Aline's, and remained there by myself, rushing to the window, as the time drew near, every time a carriage drew up before the house, and dreading to see the gilt chair behind it. It was the longest two hours and a half I ever spent in my life. At last, when I was not on the look-out for it, a carriage came rumbling in under the *porte-cochère*. A few seconds more, and the door-bell sounded. They had come back; but how? I dared not open the door and look. If she was cured, and able to walk in, a joyful cry would soon tell me of the event. I listened with a beating heart. There was a dead silence, and then the heavy tramp of feet crossing the *salon* and entering Aline's room. I waited a few minutes, still not daring to go out, when Madame André opened the door and beckoned to me.

'Come, she is asking for you,' she said.

There was no need to put any questions. I went in alone, and there, on the bed she had quitted a little while since, so full of buoyant hope, lay Aline, just as she had left it.

'Well, *ma petite*,' she exclaimed, in a voice that sounded strangely exulting, 'you see I am back again; the miracle has been performed!'

Her black eyes were shining; she was slightly flushed. '*My God! she has gone mad!*' was the thought that flashed through me. I suppose I looked terrified, and thus betrayed what was in my mind, for she said quickly,

'I am not mad. I have been mad for some time past, but I am quite sane now; I never was more so in my life. I tell you the miracle has been performed. Not the one I asked, but a greater and a better one. I was blind, stone blind, *ma petite*, and God has given me sight! I had a bandage over my eyes, and He has torn it off. I am ready to die to-morrow, this moment if He wishes it. As to my children, I have no longer the smallest anxiety about them. God wants no one to do His work. He can save and guard without me the souls He created without me. It was all an aberration of self-love, an infatuation of pride. Well, He has cured me of it! While I was praying before the relics, I felt the scales falling from my eyes as palpably as if my wounds were being closed up. The other would not have been a greater miracle. O, the mercy of our God! Only think if He had let me die in my blindness! If I had died with that blasphemous pride in my heart!'

The tears were streaming down her cheeks; her soul seemed moved to its very depths. She looked to me like a creature in an ecstasy. And so in truth she was; in an ecstasy of gratitude for the mercy that had wrought this wonder in her, and saved her by a sweeter miracle than the one she had so passionately implored.

God does nothing by halves. The cure He condescended to work in His servant was as complete as it was kind. From that day to the day of her death, which took place about six weeks later, Aline never wavered once in the act of self-abandonment she had made in the church of the Rue de Sèvres. Her one desire henceforth was to detach herself from life and all its ties. She permitted herself no tender adieux to her children, those idols that had stood so long between her faith and its centre; she contented herself with writing a few lines of farewell to them which they received after the hand which had traced them was at rest. I do not recollect the whole, but the spirit which suffused that last message is still fresh in my memory with some of the principal passages. After a few impressive words, recommending the poor to her children, reminding them that God has, in a certain degree, made our mercy to those suffering ones the measure of His mercy to us, 'Come to Me; because when I was hungry you fed Me, when I was houseless you took Me in,' she continued: 'Remember these words, my children, so as never to lose the merit of your almsgiving; but, at the same time, I trust that your hearts will always feel the need to make others happy.'* She spoke of the shortness of life,

* It sounds more tenderly expressive in French: 'J'espère que vos cœurs auront toujours besoin de faire des heureux.'

and the folly of attaching ourselves to earthly happiness, and then added : ' Our days of suffering are our best and happiest days, and when we find ourselves on our deathbed our only regret is that we have so few of them to offer to the divine mercy. Bear this in mind, my beloved ones, when the cross is pressing on you. In case I should not be able to bless you at the last moment, I give you my blessing now. Receive it in the name of the living God ; may His blessing be ever upon you, and may you ever prove yourselves worthy of your glorious title of Christians !'

One crowning mercy awaited Aline at the end. She had always expressed a great dread of dying without Extreme Unction, while, at the same time, her desire to reserve the magnificent graces of the Sacrament to the very last moment, made her reluctant to receive it an hour before it was absolutely necessary. No new sympton appeared to indicate that the supreme moment was nearer than usual, when, on the 20th of June, early in the morning, the Sister who had dressed the wounds ran in to Madame André, exclaiming :

'The end is coming, madame ! The wounds are bleeding. We must send for M. l'Abbé ; there is no time to lose !'

A messenger was despatched, and the Abbé V—— returned with him. On being told that he had come, and for what purpose, Aline evinced some surprise, and it was after some hesitation that she acquiesced, observing :

'If I have still a few weeks to live, it is a pity.'

The holy oils were administered in the presence of her mother and her children.

On leaving the room after the ceremony, the Abbé V—— exclaimed :

'What a brave soul! I never saw any one make a sacrifice to God with such an *élan* of generosity. Her only regret is that she has so little to offer Him. And yet, poor child, life has strong ties for her!'

It was about a quarter to eleven when he left the house. Aline remained in silent prayer for some ten minutes after his departure ; then she suddenly began to wander, and, as the clock struck eleven, she was quite delirious. The agony had begun, and she never afterwards regained consciousness ; at least she never spoke consciously ; though just at the end we fancied, from the movement of her hand, that she was trying to strike her breast, while her eyes sought the crucifix, and remained fixed on it till she breathed her last.

At midnight, on the 21st of June, her spirit passed away.

You will, perhaps, care to hear how God fulfilled the trust that Aline bequeathed to His sweet Providence. Her three children are married, and to men whom she might herself have chosen from among many ; Christians, not in name only, but in truth.

Madame André still lives. But her task is done, and she looks calmly for the summons that will bid her enter into the everlasting rest which awaits those who have passed through many tribulations.

ONE OF GOD'S HEROINES.

ONE OF GOD'S HEROINES.

ONE February day in the year 1813 a child was born in Castletown, Queen's County, Ireland, and christened by the name of Maria.

Her coming was not announced by bells or bonfires, or any of those gay rejoicings which attend the children of the great on their entrance into this world, and yet she was to count amongst the greatest, amongst those who are born for a glorious mission, and who achieve it nobly in the sight of God. Men were to witness it, too; but, comparatively speaking, they would be few. Like most great works, hers was to be accomplished noiselessly, silently, in lowly places, under the shadow of humility, suffering, and sacrifice.

Maria was one of five children. Her parents, Mr. and Mrs. Kelly, were devout and fervent Catholics, bringing up their family in the love of God and the practice of all Christian virtues; hospitable, charitable, esteemed by all who knew them.

Maria's childhood passed in this quiet, happy home, like that of other children, unobserved, peacefully, joyously. Nothing as yet seemed to point her out as a future modest heroine of the faith. Her piety developed itself early, it is true, and would appear to have already clothed the little one with a sort of prestige in the eyes of her brothers and sisters, for they used to say, in speaking of her: 'We are very proud of Maria, she is so good.'

In other respects there was nothing about her that attracted particular attention. She was not a little paragon of virtue, or intelligence, or beauty. She delighted in flowers, and her chief pastime was a little garden of her own, that she watered and dug and fostered with something of that patient energy of love which was one day to flow into wider channels and fertilise a nobler soil.

When she was of an age to be sent to school her parents placed her at Mrs. Keating's boarding-school, in Dublin, an establishment that was highly thought of at that time. There were few convent schools in those days, or most likely their choice would have fallen in that direction. Maria passed several years at Mrs. Keating's, and left the school with a reputation for industry, gentleness, and docility which had endeared her to all, but shed no prophetic lustre of sainthood around her. As a little child she had been fond of saying that she would be a nun; but no particular attention had been paid to the assertion, it being a very common one amongst Catholic children. She had ceased to repeat it as emphatically as formerly, perhaps because the project had sunk more deeply into her mind, and the dream was gradually shaping itself into a design.

The home that she returned to was still a singularly bright and pleasant one. A priest* who was a frequent guest there at this period gives us a charming picture of Maria in the midst of it. He was quite a young man, fresh from the seminary, where he had been taught, as part of his theology, that the world was a den of wickedness, full of roaring lions and subtle foxes, and snares and pitfalls, for those who are striving to save their souls. But all this salutary teaching received a practical denial in Mr. Kelly's house. 'It was a little Paradise,' he tells us, recalling tenderly those young impressions. 'I never witnessed anywhere more sterling piety or a greater excellence of virtue than I saw practised by those estimable people.' This piety entered into

* Very Rev. Canon Pope, Dublin.

every part of their daily lives, and manifested itself with a simplicity that reminds one of the annals of the early Christians.

Mr. Kelly had the genial hospitality peculiar to his nation. He loved to see his friends gathered round his table, but their presence never interfered with the devout customs of the family. Every evening, regularly, after dinner, one of his daughters read aloud some chapter from a spiritual book, most frequently from the *Lives of the Saints;* and our narrator remembers, more than once, seeing the tears stream down Maria's face as she read or listened to some touching passage about the sufferings of the martyrs or the sublime heroism of their virtues.

She had taken charge of the altar-linen in company with some other young ladies, and the service was a source of much pleasure to her. She taught the Catechism to the children of the poor, and was assiduous in visiting the sick. Her life, on the whole, would seem to have been a very fitting preparation for the novitiate of a Sister of Mercy.

After some years passed at home, she went to reside with one of her brothers who was living in Limerick, and while there her piety received a fresh and vigorous impulse. The idea of the religious life, which she had vaguely aspired to from her childhood, became now so strong that it was evident she must soon put it into execution. The final step was, however, preceded by long and severe interior trials—doubt, anxiety, passionate desire, alternating with heart-sinkings and sudden recoil. She could not fix her choice upon any particular order or community; each in turn attracted, but none decided her. In this trying ordeal, which is almost the inevitable precursor of every true and solid vocation to the perfect life, Maria sought strength in the intercession of the Mother of God and the prayers of the poor. She looked upon the poor as her best friends, not in the sentimental sense in which we are all ready enough to call them so, but personally and practically. She had made it her joy to serve them, to help them, to befriend them in sickness and in health, and she looked confidently to them now to help her, to prove their friendship to her, by praying her through this difficulty, and bringing her from darkness and distress to the peace and light of God's will. The poor did not prove ungrateful, neither did God betray her humble trust in them. Maria, in looking back on this painful crisis always said she felt it was the prayers of the poor that had borne her through it, and obtained light and strength for her to follow her vocation.

The Institute of the Sisters of Mercy had been recently founded in Ireland, and was working with all the fervour of a new foundation.

Maria's choice finally settled here. On the 23d of February 1838 she entered the Convent of our Lady of Mercy in Carlow, being then in her twenty-fifth year. The term of the novitiate passed quickly, and on the 11th of June of the following year the novice made her vows. During the Retreat that preceded her profession, she is described by one of those who shared her meditative solitude as 'looking very grave, but so happy'—two words that convey accurately enough the abiding expression of her countenance, at once earnest and bright.

Let us look at her for a moment as she was on entering the convent, before discarding for ever the trappings of this world.

In person she was slightly above the middle height; her features were regular, soft in their outline, and beautiful in colouring; her eyes were large and full, and readily suffused with tears that had their source in the extreme tenderness of her heart; the forehead, which was about to disappear under the religious dress, was lofty and broad, indicating thought and observation; the small well-cut mouth was mobile and firm, and had a smile that won its way to your heart; her teeth were beautiful, perfectly regular, and white as ivory, and showing very fully when she laughed—a circumstance that gave an indescribable brilliancy to her countenance in laughter. Such was Maria on the day that she knelt as a bride of Heaven at the altar. She might have been a happy bride in this world, had she so wished it. One had tried for the prize who was worthy of it perhaps, as men go, but he had failed; the young heart was not to be lured from its allegiance to the Divine Lover to whom she had dedicated her life.

Her name henceforth is Sister Mary Teresa. We perceive something of a kindred likeness to her seraphic namesake stealing over the young Sister of Mercy; a likeness that deepens as time goes on; we see something of the great Carmelite's unbroken union with God in the midst of external activity, her burning thirst for souls and untiring zeal in their service.

Sister Mary Teresa was at once placed on the list of visitors to the poor, and the way in which she performed this duty was from the first a subject of edification to those who accompanied her, the rule of the Institute being that the Sisters always go two together on the visitation. She was remarkable for that tender personal attachment to the poor which is one of the characteristics of the Saints. They were to her the living representatives of Jesus Christ, and faith made them sacred to His spouse; it pleaded for their foolishness and obliterated their faults, while it magnified their virtues and glorified their sufferings. Nothing could surpass the grace and sweetness of Sister Mary Teresa's manner towards them. Whatever she gave, whatever she did for a poor person, was invested with a charm that called out double the gratitude another would have received. 'It was not so much what she bestowed or what she did for the poor people that seemed to affect them,' says one of her Sisters; 'it was her way of doing and giving : the tenderness with which she offered an alms seemed to double its value. She had a way of comforting, too, that acted like a charm ; even when she was obliged, as was often the case, to reprimand them for their sad improvidence, want of cleanliness, &c., she had a bashful way of doing it that disarmed anything like resentment, making them *feel* that it was painful to her, that she was performing a duty solely for God and in His presence.'

Young as she was, her courage and that indescribable halo that surrounds holiness enabled Sister Mary Teresa to go everywhere, to associate with the strangest people.

Startling stories are told of some of her early campaigns amongst the wretched population where her labours chiefly lay. She soon earned a reputation for zeal and fearlessness—'pluck,' as the expressive familiar term is—that made her an object of general admiration and respect, while it brought upon her the most unlikely missions for a Sister of Mercy.

She one day received private information to the effect that a gang of very dangerous men, gamblers by trade, had come to the town, and were making terrible havoc amongst the young men, beguiling many respectable young fellows from their honest drudgery with the vain hope of sudden gain. Sister Mary Teresa never rested till she found out the head-quarters of the gang, and then she determined to go herself and make a descent upon them. It was on a Sunday morning immediately after breakfast. She selected for her companion, with permission, a Sister whose courage she knew she could trust, and the two sallied forth to beard the lion in his lair. Their walk led them through the dirtiest and poorest part of the town; they came at last to a back street, at the end of which was a disreputable-looking 'old-clothes' shop, with cast-off garments of every description hanging from the walls. The whole aspect of the place was enough to make a bold heart quail; but Sister Mary Teresa was fear-proof. Her companion was beginning to tremble a little as the crisis approached, but she pressed her arm and whispered cheerfully, 'Now, don't be frightened; they are here.' She entered the shop, quietly opened a door at the back of it, and stood on the threshold in the presence of the gamblers. It was a ghastly and painful scene; the daylight, struggling feebly in through a paper-patched window, showed the men seated in groups at separate tables, with cards and dice in their hands, their haggard countenances telling plainly enough that they had spent the night at their unhallowed occupation. They were not only taken aback by the unexpected presence of the two nuns, they were seized with shame. A dead silence followed the apparition, and no one had the courage to break it. At last Sister Mary Teresa did. We cannot reproduce her words, but her companion remembers to this day the thrill they sent through her. Sister Mary Teresa was by nature diffident almost to a fault, but on occasions like the present she was bold as any man. There was, indeed, something of the warrior about her when the honour or service of her Lord was at stake; self and all natural feeling then disappeared completely, her manner grew inspired, and her language rose to real eloquence. She upbraided the assembled gamblers with their wicked and disgraceful calling, at this moment doubly guilty from its desecration of the holy Sabbath peace; she reproached them with doing the devil's work in ensnaring souls to ruin— ruin in this life and the next; she depicted in fiery colours the miserable fate that, even in this world, awaits the gambler—poverty, humiliation, the contempt of all honest men. No one interrupted her by so much as an exclamation, until at last the leader of the gang was so much overcome by the picture that he sprang to his feet, rushed past the two nuns, and hurried out of the place. No one else stirred, but many of them began to show signs of emotion; some shed tears. When Sister Mary Teresa saw this, her tone at once changed from severity to gentleness; she ceased to threaten, and, appealing to their better instincts, reminded them of the goodness and mercy of the God they were outraging, of how He longed to save them, of the joy it would be to His Sacred Heart if they forsook their wicked courses, and like prodigal sons returned to Him and asked to be forgiven. The men could bear it no longer; they cried out that they would return, that with God's help they would amend and lead better lives for the future.

The leaders of the gang left the town immediately, and many of the young men, who had been their dupes for a while, returned to their honest employment, blessing the brave nun who had rescued them before it was too late.

Such traits become really astounding when we hear it emphatically repeated by all who knew her that timidity was one of the most striking features in Sister Mary Teresa's character.

'She was as timid as a child,' says one who knew her all her life; 'she had the simplicity of a child. There was something almost infantine about her; and yet when it was a question of preventing an offence against God, of saving a soul, no matter what the dangers or the difficulties, she rose up like a lioness defending her young. Nothing daunted her.'

The nuns used frequently to observe to each other what a different being she appeared on these occasions from what she was in the midst of them in her convent. 'She was so timid in her manners,' says one of them, 'and so sweet and simple, always effacing herself and putting others forward, always ready to appeal and to defer to their judgment, making herself of no account. But on the visitation she was a different person altogether; there she spoke with strength and feeling; her language, her manner, unconsciously to herself, rose to declamation. When there was a soul to be won to God, or terrified by His judgments, she spoke like one on fire with zeal.'

Her health was good in those early days, and she did not spare it. She walked herself off her feet. All weathers were alike to her; the cold, wet, and wind of winter and the burning heat of summer found her tramping through the streets and across the fields on her service of love. The excessive tenderness of her feet was a source of constant suffering to her, and might have justified her in shortening her walks, but it never did; she was not content with visiting in the town, but extended her mission often far beyond it, trudging ankle-deep in the mud through fields and lanes to some wretched hovel where a mother was watching by a sick child, or a wife by a husband's bed of fever. It was as much as the bravest of her companions could do to keep up with her in these expeditions. With permission she frequently sacrificed the hard-earned rest of the recreation hour to prolong her interminable search after sinners and sick people. Sometimes, in the sultry heat of the summer, her Sisters, in order to make her spare herself a little, would reproach her for being absent from them during the one hour they were free to enjoy her. She would accept the reproach with a smile; but she saw through it, and would answer with simplicity,

'Yes, I ought to be home sooner; but, O my darlings' (a familiar term of endearment she was fond of using to them), 'if you knew what a joy it is to snatch a poor soul from the devil! Only think, if sometimes we can prevent *one* mortal sin from being committed! By and by, when you have, all of you, got poor drunkards to look after, you will know what it is, and how little one feels the fatigue, or the inconvenience, or *anything*, if only one can do some little thing for our good God.'

It used to be said of Sister Mary Teresa that she had a particular knack of reclaiming inveterate drunkards; the 'knack' lay probably in her intense horror of the sin of intemperance, and the force with which her love of God enabled her to convey this horror to its unhappy victims. It is certain that God blessed her efforts in this line with marvellous success. For one thing, she had no fear of drunkards, and it is worthy of note that never in any single instance did one of those whom she admonished fail in respect to her by so much as an unbecoming word in her presence.

As we watch the young Sister of Mercy moving fearless and unharmed amidst the dens and purlieus where the very scum of the population were congregated, we are reminded of many a poetic legend ; of Una taming the lion, of the Lady who trusted the sons of Erin, and walked through the land with her golden wand, subduing rough hearts to reverence, and better guarded by her maiden purity and the chivalrous spirit of her countrymen than by a train of armed warriors.

Along with her external service, Sister Mary Teresa had the charge of distributing soup every day to the poor who came to the Convent. She had also twelve poor old men to serve daily, and she found a special delight in the duty, waiting on them as if they were in reality the twelve Apostles whom they represented in her eyes.

There is no place in a Sister of Mercy's life for squeamishness, either moral or physical, and Sister

Mary Teresa was as free from it as love and humility could render her; but this freedom did not exclude a natural and ineradicable love of cleanliness, and she perhaps gave no greater proof of her love of 'God's blessed poor' than the sacrifice of personal neatness in their service. The dispensing of the soup was fatal to this; her habit, from being splashed with the hot liquid, became at last so impregnated with grease that the nuns used to invite her to give it a good sharp boil, declaring 'it would make capital soup by itself.' She would laugh merrily, observing how 'one forgot everything in the pleasure of seeing those dear poor,' and then would add penitently, 'but it is not right to have one's habit in such a pickle; a religious should always be neat, out of respect to our holy state.'

More heroic opportunities than the soup caldron were not wanting to the spouse of Christ for the immolation of nature and its fastidious shrinkings. She performed the most disgusting offices for the sick, not only without reluctance, but with a joyous alacrity that made them look upon her as a saint.

One of her companions relates that she accompanied Sister Mary Teresa one day to a wretched hovel where an old woman was dying of a terrible malady; her body was covered with sores, while neglect and dirt had brought the poor creature to a condition that was positively loathsome to behold. The miserable bed, the floor, the whole surroundings were indescribable.

Sister Mary Teresa gave her the medicine and food they had brought, and instead of then leaving the place, as her companion expected, she proposed to wash the poor woman; 'and she performed the office with as much tenderness and respect as if she had been doing it for a queen, and as if the horrible duty had been the most agreeable pastime.' On leaving the hovel she turned to her companion and said, with a coaxing smile, 'You won't say anything about it at home, dear.'

If there was a cancer to be dressed, she did it with the same affectionate eagerness, as if it were a task she quite enjoyed, never failing to repeat the injunction, 'Don't tell them at home.' It was not to be expected this would always be obeyed.

For years after her holy death the poor still spoke of Mother Mary Teresa's kindness to them; they would tell 'how fond she was of them,' and 'what a sweet smile she had, God bless her!' One poor woman expressively describes the spiritual beauty of her countenance by the remark that 'shure God Almighty was between her eyes!'

Sister Mary Teresa had been little more than a year professed when she was chosen to found a house of the Institute in Wexford.

She was young for so arduous and responsible a mission, but she was already ripe in spiritual wisdom, and had given proofs of virtue and courage far beyond her years. She, however, was blind to this, and it was in trembling humility that she accepted the burden obedience laid upon her and went forth, at the age of seven-and-twenty, from the shelter of her Convent home to pitch her tent amongst strangers, and with the bare necessaries of life to begin with.

The new house was placed under the protection of the grand Archangel St. Michael, and the nuns entered Wexford on the 8th of December 1840. Their journey thither was effected under characteristic circumstances. Sister, henceforth Mother, Mary Teresa had been appointed Superior of the little community, which consisted of one professed, a novice, and a lay-Sister. They were accompanied by the Rev. Father Maher and two elder religious, who went to cheer the missionaries and help them over the difficulties of their installation. The party left Carlow under a threatening sky, but as they proceeded the wind rose, and the rain came down in torrents, and by the time they had got close to Enniscorthy it blew a hurricane ; the horses could hardly keep on their feet, and at last one of them backed into a ditch and could not get out of it. The wind was so fierce it was impossible for the travellers to alight and take refuge in a cabin, so the coachman got down, and, leaving his horses in charge of a poor man who happened to be passing at the moment, he went on foot to Enniscorthy to beg for the loan of a horse to pull the nuns out of the ditch. The help was readily obtained, and after two hours spent in that perilous and uncomfortable position, the Sisters were extricated, and with Father Maher, arrived at the house of the Right Rev. Dr. Keating, where they met with a hospitable welcome. They passed the night under his lordship's roof, and went forth next day to their new home at Wexford.

It sounds like derision to apply the term 'home' to a roof and four walls, so bare that, the night of their arrival, one of the priests had to go round the town begging for some blankets for the two visitor nuns, who had come unexpectedly, a few kitchen utensils, a few articles of delf, &c. One brass candlestick, which was made much of as a most valuable donation, is still preserved as a memento of those happy hard times. For they were happy in spite of their many privations, in spite of the intense cold, which was a terrible trial during that unusually severe winter; the water was frozen thick in their cells every morning, although the Sisters filled their jugs the last thing at night. In those early times they had to go out to sleep, their cells being in a house at the other side of the yard; the kitchen did duty as a refectory; the establishment contained four chairs, which the Community carried about the house, up-stairs and down-stairs, according as they wanted them.

As to their food, it is needless to add it was frugal and scanty in the extreme; the Sisters lived, in fact, pretty much like the birds of the air, taking thankfully whatever Providence sent, taking it merrily when He sent nothing.

The two elder religious remained in Wexford for a short time to assist the new-comers in getting their little Convent into some sort of shape, and then, the mission being fairly started, they took leave of them.

Those who know anything of similar undertakings will not accuse us of exaggeration when we say that the establishing of a new foundation under circumstances like the present is about as painful and arduous a task as can fall to the lot of any one. We must remember, too, that even in Catholic Ireland things have changed very much within the last five-and-thirty years, and that Mother Teresa's venture in 1840 involved an amount of courage and patience which her happier successors of the present day can scarcely realise. The population were not hostile, but they were indifferent; they did not understand Sisters of Mercy, so they did not welcome them; with few exceptions they left them to do the best they could for themselves, without offering the least help or sympathy. But God came to their rescue, and proved once more how well and abundantly His love provides for those who for His sake leave all things and trust to Him alone. Foremost amongst the many blessings granted to the missionaries at this period may be counted two friends. One was the Very Rev. James Canon Lacy, P.P. of Gorey, then C.C. of Wexford; and Mr. Richard Devereux, a rich and charitable merchant of the town. Nothing could exceed the kindness of both to the poor little Community. To mention either of those names is to call up gratitude and love too deep for praise in the memory of those whom their friendship sustained and cheered through those dark days and the brightening years that followed. Canon Lacy was a father to the nuns—such a father as a good priest can prove to a young community struggling on through poverty and loneliness. Mr. Devereux was a brother who placed his heart, his time, his purse at their disposal, and only complained because they used all three too sparingly.

For, with all their gratitude, Mother Teresa and her valiant little group of missionaries loved the cross too well to let it be too quickly lifted off their shoulders; they had chosen a hard service for their Lord's sake, and they grudged to see the thorns brushed aside and the stony path made soft. Poverty was so sweetened by love, that the empty cupboard, the cheerless hearth, the unfurnished cell had lost their terrors. Then Mother Teresa's natural gaiety and energy bore herself and her children buoyantly over everything. Nothing daunted, or baffled, or disheartened her. Badly lodged and perished as they were, they went about in rain, frost, and snow for hours every day, attending all the sick people they could hear of, and soon there was not a sick person in the whole town whom they were not made to hear of. By degrees they began to reap some sweet fruits of these labours; the poor soon came to love them, the rich to admire and respect them; in a little while the tiny seed sprang up, and the tree was broad enough for many to come and rest beneath its shade.

There was little rest for those who planted it. Their lives were an unbroken round of toil; the sick and the poor came first and claimed the largest share of their devotion, but no one was excluded; the Sisters of Mercy were at the beck of everybody; neither class nor creed made any difference.

Mother Teresa devoted herself now, as in the early days of her dedication, to the visitation of the sick poor. She loved the poor personally, as we have said; it was a pleasure and a delight to her to be with them, to talk to them, to listen to them. There was no repugnance to be overcome; love for the destitute and suffering was a natural instinct with her, an inborn sympathy, just as the love of Nature, of music, or warfaring is with others. This gives us the secret in a great measure of the extraordinary influence she obtained over them. Only persuade the poor that you are fond of them, and you can do anything with them. Many a droll story is told of Mother Teresa's conquests in this line. She went one day to see a poor woman, named Waters, who was dying. She had known her some years before, but the wretched condition in which the poor creature now was, more perhaps than the lapse of time, effaced all remembrance of her in Mother Teresa's mind. The latter, however, had scarcely said a few words when the poor woman recognised her voice, and cried out in a kind of rapture,

'Ah, thin, and is it yourself, Mrs. Kelly? Shure it was myself that loved you, and you loved my son Tom above all the young men in Carlow—the heavens be his bed! But when he died, my poor heart broke, and everything slipped from me!'

We have alluded already to the courage Mother Teresa could display when the service of souls demanded it. Some years after she left her old home in Carlow, she went back there on a visit, and it so happened that just then a man was lying in the prison of the town under sentence of death. They were praying hard for him at the Convent, but so far he had shown no signs of repentance. Mother Teresa at once proposed to go and see him, and try to win him to God and to the thought of his poor soul. What was not her horror, on entering the condemned cell, to behold in the convict one whom years ago she had known well as a little boy, and instructed for his First Communion! She knew him at once, and was terribly overcome.

'O Keilahan!' she cried, 'is this where I find you?'

The poor fellow recognised her voice, and burst into tears. From that moment his heart was changed, he gave signs of the deepest sorrow for his crime; and she who had prepared him for his innocent First Communion had the consolation of assisting him to prepare for the last, which he made in sentiments of sincere penitence, passing full of hope from the gallows into the presence of that Judge whose mercy overrules the justice of our earthly tribunals.

Many a comical incident came to enliven these more tragic ones in Mother Teresa's experience; for none enjoyed a joke more than she, or was readier to see the humorous side of a situation, or a character.

There was a woman named Madge Farrell, known to the Sisters. She was quite a celebrity in her way, and bore a sort of family likeness to her celebrated namesake of Rob Roy memory. Madge made her living by taking in lodgers; she was nominally a Protestant; but when a lodger fell ill, she insisted immediately on his seeing the priest. She always went to fetch him herself, striding into the sacristy with a stand-and-deliver air, scorning all ceremony, such as a knock or 'by your leave,' and commanding, rather than requesting, one of the clergy to come and attend to her lodger. The temptation to draw her out was sometimes irresistible.

'Well, Madge, we are glad to see you,' one of the reverend gentlemen would say; 'one of these days you'll be wanting us for yourself, eh? You'll send for me, I'll be bound?'

'Maybe I will, and maybe I won't; but the devil thank you for coming if I do!' would be Madge's retort. 'You must come when you're sent for!'

Her own turn did come at last, and the poor eccentric creature expressed in her wild incoherent way a wish to die a Catholic. A priest was summoned, and Mother Teresa went to instruct her and prepare her for the Sacraments. It was the strangest task assuredly that ever devolved on her; she had had to do with many a curious specimen of human nature, but Madge stood alone in her experience.

'Now, Madge dear, you are going to try and

examine your conscience, for you know you will have to make a general confession,' Mother Teresa began; and then added in a confidential tone: 'You used to be fond of a drop now and then; be sure to remember to tell that!'

Madge turned on her like a fury.

'What! is it Tom Kelly's daughter that's talking to me? As if I'd be entertainin' his reverence wid my drunken pranks! No, no; Madge knows her place better than that.'

It was with great difficulty she was persuaded to take another view of the case; but at last Mother Teresa succeeded, and somehow or other the examination of conscience was got through. Then came the grand affair of exciting Madge to sorrow for her sins.

'Now, Madge dear, we are going to make a good act of contrition,' said Mother Teresa: 'O my God, I am heartily sorry for all my sins.'

'Shure, and if the neighbours is to be believed,' broke in the penitent, 'I'm the biggest sinner that ever drew the breath o' life!'

The acts of Faith and Hope were got through without comment; but when it came to repeating 'and I love my neighbour as myself,' Madge had her say again:

'Bedad, and if I love them better than myself they'd be for hanging me the next minute, if they could!'

She lingered several months in great suffering, until at last, wonderfully softened, and no doubt purified by her patient endurance, poor Madge expired in Mother Teresa's arms, looking up into her face.

But it was not only great sinners and the destitute poor who were the objects of Mother Teresa's charity and zeal. Hers was one of those large hearts that know no limits, but embrace in their universal sympathy suffering of every shape and sinners of every class. The fame of her goodness and holiness had carried her name far beyond the narrow circle of her life and drew many strange petitioners to her door. The most unlikely persons came to ask her for advice and consolation. Wonderful tales are told of the devices she found in her love and wisdom for answering these appeals; but there is not a single instance on record of her having repulsed any one. Her nature was so sympathetic, that it enabled her spontaneously and without any effort to enter into the troubles and sorrows of others, no matter how far removed they might be from the range of her own experience. She could feel acutely for the trials of seculars, fathers and mothers of families, both rich and poor ; she could interest herself in the prospects and struggles of young people starting in life, and would help them to the utmost of her power by her advice, her prayers, and her influence. She felt a still tenderer interest in young girls, and would dare and bear almost anything to stand between them and harm, or to place their innocence beyond the reach of it. Her contrivances in this respect were something wonderful; she managed to protect and feed a number of young girls and keep them under her own sheltering wing until Providence opened some safe permanent abode to them. Resources never failed her ; charity like hers is contagious ; a spark of the fire that burned in her own heart fired the hearts of others ; and, whenever she was in difficulties about some act of kindness, a generous person was sure to come forward with the necessary means.

In 1865 Mr. Devereux consoled and rejoiced her by building a House of Mercy close to the Convent, where young girls of good character are taken care of while they happen to be unemployed elsewhere ; a large public laundry was established there to give them work so long as they chose to remain.

But when as, alas! it would sometimes happen, the objects of her watchfulness lost the crowning glory of their youth and fell below the pity of this world, Mother Teresa's heart was open to them with a still wider compassion. Hearts that are pure and full of the love of God have no room for scorn. The virgin spouse of Christ held out her hand in mercy to the poor degraded sister whom the honourable matron turned from in disdain. When they came to her in penitence and shame, they were received with the tenderest charity; when they fled from her, she sought them out. Many an obscure Magdalen will rise up at the last day and bless Mother Teresa before the Judgment Seat, proclaiming her the messenger of God's dear mercy to their souls.

The instruction of the ignorant, especially of adults, had a great attraction for her. She opened classes for them in the Convent and taught there herself, when she could snatch a few hours from more imperative duties. In the early days of the formation, men attended at night sent by the priests, and these Mother Teresa always instructed. It was very remarkable to see the effect of her words on the rough audience; they listened to her as if she were an angel come straight down from heaven, and on leaving the house would give vent to their feelings with characteristic emphasis : ' She bates the priests out and out, God bless her !' ' Shure, and we'd rather be listenin' to her than to Dr. Sinnott himself!' The Very Rev. Dr. Sinnott was the President of the College, a highly gifted man and a very eloquent speaker.

During the missions Mother Teresa would collect as many ignorant grown men and women as she could, and herself prepare them for the Sacraments, very often for the Sacrament of Confirmation. She went about to the lodging-houses where poor people come for a night or two, and she would use her utmost endeavours to make them go to the church and make their peace with God before leaving the town. In this way she brought many to the Sacraments who had not approached them for years.

Persons of every age and calling came to her for advice. Some sought her counsel in the great concern of their vocation, and there are not a few ministering at the altar who, when they elevate the Sacred Host, must remember Mother Teresa as the friend whose wisdom helped them to that glorious prerogative. A saintly lay-brother, who attributed his vocation in a great measure to her guidance and encouragement, wrote to her Convent on hearing of her death : ' She was my best and dearest friend! Now that she is gone, I feel a loneliness on earth which you and those who loved her well can understand.'

'She was an untiring, enthusiastic labourer in the vineyard, and had God's greater glory always and only in view,' is the testimony of one who for a long time has laboured in the Society of Jesus with the zeal of an apostle. ' Her sympathy for the suffering and afflicted was great,' writes another ; 'she would do anything for them that hands could do; but their immortal souls were her chief, her grand concern. When she found the poor neglecting their religious duties she gave them no rest till they had fulfilled them, instructing them herself, teaching them their prayers, explaining to them the nature of true contrition, its motives and effect, making light of all the difficulties that stood in the way, reminding them of the folly of being ashamed to confess, comforting them with the assurance of recovering the friendship of their merciful God as soon as they had complied with these easy conditions. And God blessed her efforts for poor sinners with wonderful success. Her zeal was far greater than her strength, although the latter, not being fettered by self-love, enabled her often to perform the spiritual and corporal works of the Institute when others less courageous would have thought it incumbent on them to rest.'

In considering the beauties of a holy soul it is difficult to say which predominates; all the virtues are akin, and they melt so imperceptibly one into the other that it is not easy to discern where one begins and the other ends. There is, nevertheless, generally a certain perfume distinctively characteristic of souls that seems to indicate the prevailing presence of some one particular virtue, just as, in a garden full of flowers, the scent of one will make itself felt above the rest. One would fancy that, from the very nature of Mother Teresa's vocation, zeal would have claimed this bright supremacy over all the sister virtues, yet those who are best qualified to form an opinion agree that it belongs to humility. The same sentiment comes spontaneously from all. 'Humility was her predominant virtue; it was quite extraordinary to see what a low opinion she had of herself, how she always contrived to keep herself out of sight and to put others forward.'

She was a woman of considerable ability; her administrative talents were of a high order; nature had endowed her largely, in mind as well as in soul. But Mother Teresa was perfectly unconscious of this; she spoke of herself, and really believed herself to be a very commonplace mediocre person. She wrote admirably, for instance; the matter was excellent, always original and well digested, and her style flowed on with a sprightly natural grace; yet Mother Teresa honestly believed her letters were not fit to be read. Like that grand soul, Mother Margaret Hallahan, she had a habit of appealing to any one who happened to be near her when she was writing, not for assistance in the spelling—her early education put that out of question —but as to how she should express herself. 'Tell me what I ought to say to so-and-so,' 'how I ought to put this,' were appeals that were frequently addressed to some young novice, who remained edified and humbled by the humility of her superior.

The same spirit of self-abasement led her to seize every opportunity of humbling herself towards the Community when it could be done without singularity, for no one had a greater horror of singularity than Mother Teresa. Once at the close of a Retreat about Christmas she was giving an instruction to the Nuns, when suddenly, as if overpowered by a sense of her own unworthiness, she broke out into vehement protestations of her nothingness in the sight of the Eternal God, and acknowledged her incapacity to have the charge of their souls with a fervour of humility that went to the hearts of all present. But this was nothing compared to what they felt on beholding their Superior prostrate herself before the crib where the little King of Bethlehem lay enthroned on His bed of straw, and, in accents broken with sorrow, implore them for His sake to forgive all the faults and the bad example she had been guilty of during the year.

It seems a foolish remark to make that Mother Teresa's humility was sincere; but there are degrees of sincerity here as elsewhere, and it would seem evident that hers bore the stamp of sincerity in a very remarkable degree. She impressed those who knew her with the feeling that she was not so much performing a deliberate act of virtue in humbling herself as giving vent to a strong inward conviction of her own inferiority. She had an intellectual belief that she was a very sinful, unintelligent, and worthless person. This it was that taught her to welcome ingratitude and insult, and even calumny, as a due. She seemed to lose sight completely of herself on such occasions, to think only of the sin that was being committed against God, and the harm the sinners were doing their own souls. 'It seemed like a sensible physical pain to her to see God offended,' says a priest who had ample opportunities of judging Mother M. Teresa.

Only a few days before her death she was attacked and gratuitously insulted by a woman who had long been the recipient of her bounty and the object of her active charity. Not content with pouring out the coarsest abuse on her benefactress, the wretched woman pushed her violently aside, cursing horribly all the while. A lady who was present at the painful scene remained lost in wonder at Mother Teresa's meekness and absence of the least personal indignation. 'But the sound of the cursing,' she said, 'seemed to go through her like a knife.' When any wrong was committed against herself or the Community, her first thought was, 'O, that our good God should be so offended !' Far from harbouring any personal resentment against the culprits, she felt grateful to them for giving her an opportunity of suffering something for God. Her deep compunction for her sins made her welcome humiliation with joy as a means of atoning for them.

It remained to the last day of her life a source

of honest surprise to Mother Teresa that she should ever have been elected Superior. Those who lived under her rule can testify to the wisdom which placed and kept her so long in that high post ; those who shared her labours can tell what courage and self-devotion and prudence she displayed throughout. *She* saw none of this. When things went well and her efforts prospered, it was due to the labours of others and the gratuitous mercy of God ; when they went ill, then it was all her fault : her unworthiness was the obstacle ; she alone was to blame for the failure. It was sometimes an amusement to her Sisters to notice the ingenuity, and at the same time the perfect *naïveté*, with which she applied this theory on occasions. For instance, if a large donation came for the poor when she was out of office, she would exclaim quite naturally : ' See how God prospers us since I am no longer Superior ! How the alms pour in ! It is easy to see I was an obstacle to many blessings.'

Examples of that taste for calumny which is the sublimest height to which humility can reach were not wanting in Mother Teresa's life. Like all humble souls, she was deeply grateful ; few things could be more painful to her natural feelings than to be accused or suspected of ingratitude. To show her a kindness, to do her a service, was to make her your debtor for life. It so happened that a priest who had shown great kindness to the Community was led to believe that Mother Teresa had used her influence unfavourably to him on a certain occasion, and he gave her to understand that he was very much disappointed and hurt by it. The whole thing was a mistake; she herself had suffered quite as much from the decision as he had, and she had only to say a word to make him see this. But though she felt the suspicion most acutely, she never spoke that word; for fifteen years she bore it in silence, merely informing one who had her confidence, that when she came to be on her deathbed she would send for the person in question, and explain to him how it had all been, adding, 'He will then pray the more fervently for my soul.' Her last illness was too sudden to admit of her doing this; but the message was transmitted after her death through her Superior, and the revelation it contained filled with sorrow the person who had unwittingly misjudged her, and raised Mother Teresa still higher in his esteem.

She was a model of religious obedience. Though so long Superior that authority might seem to have become natural to her, she laid aside every shadow of it the moment her term of office expired. It seemed a satisfaction to her to slip off the burden and dwindle into insignificance as far as she possibly could, making herself as small as the youngest postulant, deferring to everybody's judgment, as if she had no longer any right to an opinion of her own.

One of her Superiors relates that conversing with Mother Teresa one day on the different standards that souls adopt on embracing the religious life, she asked her what hers had been. They were standing before a roaring fire at the moment. 'Mine,' said Mother Teresa, 'was that if a Superior told me to put my hands into that grate and gather up the live coals and carry them to the top of the house, I would do it immediately.'

'Her obedience was never put to so severe a test,' adds the narrator, 'but, as far as opportunity required it, she carried out this standard to its most rigorous perfection.' 'Her prompt, docile, simple obedience was most humbling to us while we had charge of the Community,' declare two of her Superiors; 'she had a noble mind, capacious as her heart; but when we consulted her on any important matter she gave her opinion with great diffidence, always putting it as if not from herself, but as what she believed so-and-so would be likely to advise, or as what was done in such and such a Community, almost invariably adding, " But you are best judge ;" she had the lowliest opinion of her own judgment.'

It was doubtless from constant meditation on the Passion of our Blessed Lord, Mother Teresa's special attraction, that she drew that deep and generous love of the Cross that all who approached her closely detected and admired. She once confessed to a religious that her great spiritual ambition was to arrive at having a love of being spoken ill of; a confession which gives us the secret of many things which at the time appeared incomprehensible to those who witnessed them. She would deliberately try to pass for an imperfect religious and a weak-minded person—a practice of humility which nevertheless was rigidly controlled by her innate simplicity and her horror of anything that verged on affectation or singularity ; she never made such opportunities, but they were irresistible when they came in her way.

'Sensitive as she was by nature,' says one of her Superiors, 'I have seen her positively exult with joy when the cross was presented to her.'

Poverty is the badge and glory of the true religious. In an Order such as the Sisters of Mercy there would seem but little scope for the breach of it ; yet where all were poor, Mother Teresa contrived to be poorest. She never would have anything new when it was possible to avoid it; she would lay hold of the patched and threadbare clothes of the Nuns, and things that were cast off as impossible for further wear and set aside she would solicit for her own use. This particular practice of poverty must have been a severe trial to one who was naturally neat to daintiness. The same spirit of detachment pervaded all her actions ; she never made a choice of anything, but took haphazard whatever came first. She liked to see her Sisters acting the same way ; as when beads were blessed, for instance, she would have them put out their hand and take, without selection, the first that came.

Self-denying and mortified as she was herself, Mother Teresa was prone to be over-indulgent to others. Her kindness to the sick was carried to the verge of weakness. She filled the office of infirmarian to the Community for a long time, and many grateful memories are laid up in the hearts of those who enjoyed her motherly care during that period. Mortification and asceticism entered very little into her rule over the sick-room. One of her Sisters relates an instance of Mother Teresa's gentle forbearance towards herself when being nursed by her in a slight illness. It was in the early days at Carlow, when the Community was too poor to supply all necessaries, much less delicacies, to its sick members. Those were the days, too, of black draughts and powders and other horrible institutions, now become matters of history to our advanced civilisation. The invalid had been condemned to one of these dreadful panaceas, and Mother Teresa was administering comfort after the dose in the shape of a little lemon-juice and sugar in a metal spoon; the metal was discoloured from constant use, for there was only one spoon in the infirmary, and the fastidious palate of the young novice turned from it naturally enough with disgust. 'It was enough to poison one,' she declared, 'to put such a black thing into one's mouth.' Mother Teresa, instead of rebuking the childish pettishness, apologised in the humblest way for the nasty appearance of the spoon, explaining that there was only one and she had not time to polish it. 'I shall never forget how her humility humbled me, and how thoroughly ashamed I felt,' said the culprit, writing of it long afterwards.

She was as watchful of the health of the Nuns as any mother, and almost as anxious. A Sister happened to cough several times in choir one evening, and that night, just as she had lain down, Mother Teresa came into her cell with a bowl of hot gruel. 'Take this, my darling, it will do you good,' she said; 'you must get rid of that cough.' The Nun said it was the first intimation she had of its existence. Sisters of Mercy have little time or thought to spare on their own ailments.

'She was more than a mother to us,' says one of her religious; 'she took more care of us than the most ingenious self-love could suggest.'

She always took care to have a good bright fire in the Community-room to cheer the Sisters on the winter evenings after their hard day's work. In wet weather, when they came home from the Visitation or out-school she would hasten herself to help them off with their damp clothes, and insist on feeling with her own hands if their feet were wet; in such circumstances a Sister relates that on one occasion she saw her go on her knees and rub them with spirits lest a cold should be the result. There was no thought of maintaining her dignity as Superior; the mother's love overruled all such considerations, and truly it brought its reward, for never was a Superior more deeply reverenced than this self-forgetting, humble, tender-hearted mother. When the ground was frozen and slippery, she had list or strips of cloth fastened on the Sisters' boots to prevent their falling on the ice, as she once did herself.

She delighted to see them merry at recreation, and encouraged the young to give free play to their fun and high spirits. She was of a cheerful, even gay, disposition herself, and a most entertaining companion, yet there was always an air of recollection about her, 'as if she never lost sight of the presence of God,' her Sisters used to say. While joining in the laughter and whatever amusement was going on at recreation with as much apparent zest as the youngest of them, there was always 'that something' that seemed to remind you her heart was with her treasure, far away.

In the midst of the most distracting external work her soul seemed as peacefully united to God as in the act of prayer. This close sense of His presence sometimes so abstracted her from outward things that involuntarily she betrayed herself, and ejaculatory prayers would escape from her, as if she were alone; generally they were acts of contrition and humility.

On the eve of Communion-days the Sisters whose cells communicated with hers used to hear her praying aloud in this way during the night.

Some of her favourite aspirations, uttered thus when all around was silent and dark, impressed themselves so distinctly on a listener's memory that she wrote them down. We subjoin some few that are characteristic of Mother Teresa's devotional feelings:

'O Eternal Father! I offer you all the acts of love produced by the adorable Heart of Jesus on earth, especially during the hours that He was agonising on the Cross.'

'O my God! I offer Thee the profound annihilations of Jesus humbled and crucified.'

'O my merciful God! I put my *whole* trust in Thee. I firmly hope for mercy, grace, and salvation from Thee, my good God, through Jesus Christ my Saviour!'

'Send forth Thy holy Angels, O Lord, to prepare a dwelling for Thee in my soul.'

She knew the penitential psalms by heart, and often fell asleep reciting them. I have before me at this moment a little printed prayer of hers, worn and discoloured from constant use, which gives us a glimpse into that inner sanctuary where no human eye penetrated. We see the servant of God asking for 'the love of contempt and obscurity, infirmities, insults, and interior pains.' 'Assist me, O Jesus, to prove the sincerity of my love by mortifying, for Thy sake, my sinful inclinations, renouncing my ease and my will. Mary, my Mother, pray for me! I am absolutely destitute, but I shall become rich when thou deignest to cast on me one glance of compassion. O my Saviour! may I correspond with Thy merciful designs.'

The motto engraved on her Profession ring was, ' Lord Jesus, I am Thine! Save me!'

Ten years after the Wexford foundation Mother Teresa was deputed to establish another at Cappoquin, in the County Waterford.

Here again the story of poverty and privations gaily borne repeats itself.

The Convent of the Sisters of Mercy was the first opened in this locality, so that on their arrival there the Nuns found the poor, especially the little children, in a state of deplorable spiritual ignorance and neglect. Mother Teresa remained long enough to set the new house afloat, and then returned to Wexford, where she had been reëlected Superior.

In 1853 she founded a Branch House of the Order at New Ross, in the County Wexford. Here the first night the Nuns slept on the floor, and we are not told that their slumbers were the less sound for that penitential bed.

They opened a school at New Ross for the middle classes, as there was none such in existence under religious, and afterwards one for the poor. Mother Teresa remained about six weeks at New Ross, and then returned home, leaving the young mission under the charge of a local Superior. In 1857 this house was made a Foundation.

In 1858 another Branch House was opened under her superintendence at Enniscorthy, the Cathedral town of the diocese, and made a greater demand on her energy and persevering courage than perhaps any of the previous undertakings. The Nuns had to move from place to place five times in a few years before they secured a permanent shelter. Here, as ever, their friend Mr. Devereux came nobly to the rescue, giving 1000*l.* towards the building of a suitable convent, a donation which was followed by a very generous one from the Right Rev. Dr. Furlong, the Bishop of the diocese.

For nine years Mother Teresa continued to superintend the house at Enniscorthy, and she was repaid by seeing it prosper abundantly under her wise and active direction.

Her ardent devotion to the Holy Sacrifice made her anxious to secure to the poor at every cost opportunities of assisting at it. She never failed when attending them, in sickness or in health, to stir them up to the importance of this duty, by instructing them on the nature of Mass, its magnificent efficacy, its power to glorify God, and draw down blessings on themselves. If she suspected that they were hindered, as so many are, by shyness, because of their ragged clothes, she would provide them with good ones, so that this excuse might not deter them.

Numbers were prevented hearing Mass on Sundays at one side of the town of Enniscorthy, on account of the distance to the Cathedral. Mother Teresa resolved to build a Chapel for them outside the Convent of Mercy, the site of which she purposely selected in this poorest and most spiritually destitute locality. She succeeded; but at what a cost of toil and anxiety God alone knows. In this good work, as in so many others, she was assisted by her two staunch friends, Canon Lacy and Mr. Devereux. The little Gothic Chapel, which had involved greater trouble and sacrifice than any undertaking she had carried through, was not quite finished when she died, and one of the last acts of her life was to give up the Convent Altar to have Mass said on Christmas morning in a temporary Chapel which was to be arranged in a very poor district not far off. Perhaps the fact of the Enniscorthy

Chapel being the last work she was to do for God in this world made her, unawares, throw a kind of passionate energy into its accomplishment, for those who saw her through its progress declared that she seemed on fire with zeal about it. 'It was truly a monument of her ardent disinterested charity,' writes one who was a witness of her zeal in this last work; 'her one and only thought in its erection was the gain it would be to souls.'

There never was indeed a religious more utterly free from that kind of innocent complacency in her Order which is sometimes but a sort of personal vanity removed to a higher and purer sphere. Her first and supreme ambition was that her Order should 'get some glory for our good God,' as she lovingly put it, by helping to save souls; this was the sum-total of her desires; the material prosperity, the popularity of the Institute, all this was a matter of absolute indifference to her, except inasmuch as it tended to the furtherance of the higher end.

And now we have come to the last days of the year 1866.

Christmas, Mother Teresa's best-loved Feast of all the year, was at hand. She had prepared for it with greater fervour than ever. She was not as strong as formerly, and she spared herself less as the time went on. There was a great deal of sickness about. Cholera had broken out in the town, and though not yet raging as an epidemic, the cases were of a deadly kind, most of them proving fatal. At Wexford, not very distant, the cholera wards of the hospital were full, and the Sisters of Mercy for five weeks had been attending them. So far all had been mercifully preserved from the contagion. At Enniscorthy the pestilence was still confined to the districts where squalid poverty had prepared the way for it, and now proved its most powerful auxiliary. Mother Teresa spent much of her time in these plague-stricken hovels, 'where the air was so foul,' says the Sister who accompanied her, 'that it was worse than the most crowded cholera ward in a hospital.' Up to the day before Christmas-eve she continued to spend her mornings in this arduous service.

The Sister of Mercy's day is portioned out as follows: at 5 she rises; meditation, office, and Mass occupy till near seven; then breakfast and manual work, Spiritual Lecture in Community at 8, for half an hour, after which a certain number of the Sisters adjourn to the schools, whilst others are told off to the Visitation of the Sick until $3\frac{1}{2}$.

Vespers intervene between then and dinner, which is at 3¾; half an hour's recreation follows dinner; the life of a saint is read at 5 for half an hour in Community, the Foundress of the Order intending this as a little spiritual recreation following the labours of the day. The remainder of the evening is divided between study, office, meditation, until supper, which comes at 7, and is followed by recreation again. Night prayers are at 9, and at 9½ the day's work is over and all retire to rest.*

Besides the increased demand made upon her time and strength by the increase of sickness amongst the poor, Mother Teresa had a great deal to do in preparation for the festival. The crib had to be made ready, and its adornment was one of her greatest delights. In connection with this subject I may relate a characteristic incident. Mother Teresa's desire was that all the poor people within her range should gather round a crib; but there was one place where, owing to the laws and rules enforced, the inmates could not go out to visit the cathedral and chapels where the poor stable was represented; we cannot call it a *home*

---

* The duties and exercises of the Sisters of Mercy are the same in all countries, but the hours appointed to them vary according to the circumstances of each place.

R

for the destitute, as it is divested of all that renders home, however poor, dear and bright—kind faces and loving hearts; but it is a refuge provided by the State for those who have no shelter—the 'workhouse.' Well, this tender mother of the poor asked and obtained permission to present a figure of the Divine Infant to the chapel attached to this Institute, and because the patients confined to bed in the hospital could not visit it even there, she took the Image in her arms and went with it through the wards, gratifying the piety of the simple souls whose suffering and poverty so likened them to the little King of Bethlehem. It was reversing the procession of the Shepherds to the stable—Jesus coming to them, instead of their going to Him. Exclamations of wonder, surprise, and devotion were heard on all sides, 'O the Darlint!' 'God be praised!' &c. The very Christmas she died Mother Teresa had a Sister engaged illuminating these words on a scroll for the workhouse crib—'Dear little One! how sweet Thou art!'

But to return to the Christmas of 1866. A bazaar had recently been held for the sick and afflicted visited by the Sisters of Mercy. It was a work of great toil and anxiety for Mother Teresa, as all the arrangements, even to the smallest details, devolved on her. Her mental and bodily powers were taxed to the uttermost; but she gladly endured every fatigue in order to obtain means to relieve the suffering objects of her care. With the proceeds she was enabled to distribute an abundance of clothing, and just at this season of cold and want she was busily engaged in preparing it. It was a duty she loved above all others, and she threw her whole heart into it with lively faith. The sufferings of the poor lay heavily on that tender heart at all times, but it was downright misery to her to think of their being cold or hungry at Christmas. To see how she pleaded and toiled and stitched to provide clothes and food for them on this day, one would have supposed that some personal penalty was in store for her should any be found in want of them. She strove with her might to make the coming of the little King a day of joy to all, that His birth might light a flame on the perishing hearth and make a home in the desolate places. But what was this compared to her longing to make a home for Him in their souls, and light the flames of His love in their hearts? How she worked and prayed and wept for this—to bring home the prodigals, to soften the impenitent, to gather the forlorn little ones round His crib! Sweet, brave Mother!

In heaven, please God, those hidden triumphs of your love will be revealed to us, and, meantime, you will pray that our hearts may glow with one little spark of the fire that burned so ardently in yours.

Christmas-eve came, and all was ready; neither she nor those around her knew how ready. The altar was raised, the fagots were placed on it, the victim was at hand for the holocaust. Faithful to her life-long habit of taking every troublesome office on herself, Mother Teresa rose earliest of all the house on that happy morning, and called the Community. She joined in morning prayers, and made her meditation with the rest; but about half-past six she felt faint, left the choir, and did not return for Mass at seven. There was nothing so far to alarm her Sisters. She did not join them at breakfast, but afterwards she read her letters, and was greatly pleased with some pretty Christmas cards that some of these contained. She continued to transact the business of the house through two of the senior religious up to midday, when the symptoms suddenly assumed a more serious character, and the doctor was sent for. He ordered her to bed immediately, and said at once that the case looked very bad. A confessor was hastily summoned, as the ordinary one in attendance was absent, and the last rites of the Church were administered.

Had it come to this? A cry of agony and horror ran through the house. 'Our Mother is dying of cholera!' The Christmas joy was changed into despair, the happy Christmas carols into tears and supplications. To Mother Teresa alone the sudden message was welcome; the unbidden guest had no terrors for her; she had been watching for him these fifty years, and now he had come to take her to her Spouse; the night had fallen suddenly, but in a little moment it would be daylight.

After receiving Extreme Unction she asked her attendants to withdraw, that she might remain alone for an hour with God.

A telegram was sent to Wexford, and four of the Nuns started at once for Enniscorthy, where they arrived about six o'clock. Mother Teresa retained the full use of speech until four. Up to that time she was continually praying aloud, in the most touching and beautiful words; her aspirations breathed nothing but contrition, humility, and love; above all, love.

'O my Jesus, I love Thee, I love Thee!' she

would exclaim ; and then, turning to the religious, who never left her side, ' O, if I *could* love Him !'

'You do, dearest Mother ; you do love Him !' her companion would urge.

' Well, yes, I do, I do !' she would reply.

Her body was a prey to the violent pangs of the terrible disease, but while every limb was convulsed in agony her soul continued serenely united to God; she was writhing like a worm, yet her face preserved its sweetness, and wore the old smile that was so heartrendingly beautiful now ; she broke out every moment into transports of love, like one in an ecstasy ; those around her were almost pained, and tried to restrain her, fearing she would exhaust too quickly the little strength that yet remained. Frequently she cried out loudly, ' O God, be merciful to me !' Several times she sent the Sisters to the choir to pray that she might have a happy death and a merciful judgment. Her mind was wonderfully withdrawn from earthly concerns ; from the very first she seemed to have banished all thought of them, a circumstance that was the more remarkable in that she was at the time overwhelmed with anxiety concerning the completion of the Convent and Chapel at Enniscorthy ; but from the moment she received the last Sacraments her soul seemed lifted completely above this world. It was a source of indescribable comfort and edification to those who witnessed her calm, placid, sweet abandonment of herself to the will of God. She made the sacrifice of her life at once, without the slightest effort, like a child lying down in its mother's arms to sleep. Even the still greater, the supreme sacrifice of receiving the Viaticum, which the nature and conditions of cholera rendered it impossible to give her, was made without a murmur. There was just one exclamation of disappointment when it was announced to her, but she immediately made her act of renunciation, and never retracted it by so much as a word of regret.

The confessor who assisted her all through the last struggle declared that her soul was as detached as if it was already set free from its prison of clay; not a single tie held her back.

The only moment she gave to temporal affairs was while giving some few directions to the Sisters about the distribution of the Christmas relief; they were almost the last intelligible words she uttered; it was fitting and characteristic that they should have been about the poor in whose service she had spent and, we may truly say, sacrificed her life.

The Bishop, the Right Rev. Dr. Furlong, who

had left Wexford for Enniscorthy that day, arrived towards five, when Mother Teresa had no longer the power of speech. His dismay and grief were indescribable. He had known her for thirty years, and during that time he had seen her at work and learned to love her, as souls love who are united by the divine bond of charity. There were few on earth to whom he was more deeply attached in God. At first he was so stunned that he could not realise the danger, he could not believe in it. Soon, however, it became too apparent that the sands were fast running down, and that all that remained to him to do was to bow his head and surrender this beloved Sister in Christ crucified to the Spouse who was calling her to His embraces. When the Nuns from Wexford arrived they found the venerable prelate in their Mother's cell, kneeling by her bedside, too prostrate with grief himself to be able to offer them any consolation. Three of the Missionary Fathers were there too, and with the Bishop continued to pronounce at intervals the solemn words of absolution over the dying Nun.

One of the medical men, a Protestant, was quite overcome by the beauty of the Catholic scene, and could not refrain from expressing his admiration. His professional instinct was distressed and alarmed to see the Sisters and the priests pressing heedlessly round the pestilence-stricken patient, and in a whisper he warned them to be more prudent; but other cares were in their hearts than self-preservation. Surprised and touched by the heroic self-forgetfulness one and all displayed, he exclaimed involuntarily, 'This is truly a happy deathbed!'

The brain is often affected in cholera—I believe, indeed, that delirium is one of the afterstages of the malady—but the medical men declared there was no such symptom in Mother M. Teresa's case; her mind remained clear to the last, and the state of collapse followed quite closely on one of those transports of love and contrition we have described.

The Bishop himself recited the prayers for the agonising, but when he came to the recommendation of the departing soul, where he had to pronounce Mother Teresa's name, his voice was so choked with tears that he was obliged to pause before he could go on.

At eleven the Sisters insisted on his lordship going away for the night to take a little rest, for he had the first three Masses to celebrate in the Cathedral at early dawn, and besides he was quite worn out with fatigue and emotion. 'We cannot afford to lose both father and mother at once,' they urged, and he yielded to their filial entreaties.

The Missionary Fathers remained still watching, blessing, and absolving the soul that was about to take its flight from earth. The struggle had ceased; there was no agony, the end was soft and gentle as the falling asleep of an infant. The clock of the Cathedral struck the blessed midnight hour, and, as if she had been waiting for that signal, Mother Teresa breathed her last. She had gone to sing the *Gloria in excelsis* with the angels. How were they to sing it, those whom she had left behind, departing from their midst just as the glorious message came?

Next morning the Bishop himself announced her death from the altar. When he asked for prayers for the repose of her soul his voice faltered, a thrill of emotion ran through the congregation, there was hardly a dry eye present. The day of jubilee was changed into a day of mourning, not only in the cabins of the poor, where her bounty had spread a festive board, but in the houses of the rich, where many an aching heart had been soothed, many a stricken soul uplifted and strengthened by the departed Sister of Mercy. But it was the poor chiefly who mourned for her. They had lost a

Mother who was not to be replaced. 'She spent herself for the poor,' said the sorrowing Bishop, who announced their loss to them.

On Christmas-day they brought her back to Wexford, and whilst the remains were being borne from the Convent door to the hearse, a poor woman pushed her way up to the coffin, and, heedless of contagion, fell upon it, weeping bitterly, and calling on Mother Teresa as if she were alive and listening to her. They laid her to sleep in the little graveyard of the Convent of St. Michael's, of which for twenty-six years she had been the light and the life. The scene was beautiful, but at the same time heart-breaking. The prelate, attended by a clergyman, stood over the grave, lifting up their voices in prayer for her whom they were laying to rest; but louder than these rose the sobs of the religious who had so long been her children. And wherever the news of her death reached, the tears of the poor flowed, and on all sides were heard the lament of the widow and orphan and the blessings of the countless hearts she had taught and comforted and tended.

My little task of love is done, but I cannot close it without transcribing a few lines from the pen of one who knew and loved Mother Teresa well, and whose testimony is a far worthier panegyric than this short and inadequate record. It is from a Cistercian Monk, the Right Rev. Dr. Fitzpatrick, Abbot of Mount Melleray, and was written to the sorrowing Community in the first days of their bereavement:

'I tell you candidly I would rather *not* write to you on this occasion. I scarcely know what to say in a letter, though in conversation I could tell you much that would edify you, and give you, if possible, a still higher opinion of your most dear departed Sister.

'I never could discover a defect in her; I never perceived what I could consider the slightest venial fault; I never saw a momentary cloud passing over her countenance; I never heard a word from her that I could have wished unspoken. I never found her unrecollected. So much for what I did *not* see. A few words more upon what I *did* see. In Mother M. Teresa I saw Christian and religious perfection, such as I should wish to see in every Nun, not only of your admirable Order, but of every Order, whether active or contemplative. In her I found fully realised my notions of human perfection. In her presence I never could forget the presence of God. The very mention of her name will, to the last moment of my life, call forth in shadowy array before my mind all those virtues and perfections which constitute that most lovely, most beautiful, and most delicate of all God's works, the "Nun sanctified."'

Laus Deo.

MONSEIGNEUR DARBOY.

MONSEIGNEUR DARBOY.

I AM not going to preface the history of his death by a sketch of his life; merely by an incident in it which he related to me himself, one morning that I went to see him with two friends, at his Palace in the Rue de Grenelle, now many years ago.

The conversation turned at first, and dwelt for some time, on the topics of the day, political and otherwise; and then fell upon a question which had been warmly discussed of late amongst a small circle of earnest and suffering spirits, namely, whether or not we should recognise in heaven those whom we had known and loved on earth. One of the company expressed, half-doubtingly, a hope that we should. I can recall, as vividly as if he were before me now, the bright expression of the Archbishop's face, and the sudden vivacity of his manner as he turned to the speaker who had appealed to him for a solution; he had been leaning back in his armchair,—that great tabernacle of a *fauteuil* that made the spare, ascetic figure look even smaller than it was,—and suddenly sitting up, and raising his hand with a quick emphatic gesture, he exclaimed:

'*Comment donc!* It is not alone that we shall know each other, but we shall know each other far better than we did on earth; we shall read the secrets of one another's hearts, those that we had here, for *là haut*,' pointing to the sky, 'there will be no more secrets. And what sweet and wonderful revelations await us! We shall discover miracles without number that have landed many souls in heaven, but never been chronicled on earth; we shall learn how such a crime that we were on the point of committing, and did not, such an act of virtue that we were about to forego for lack of strength, and did not, were all owing to the prayer of some one who loved us, who was pleading and suffering for us, and saving our soul while we were losing it; we did some trifling service to a humble friend, a servant, a beggar perhaps, to whom we dropped an alms on a winter's day, and they paid us back in a blessing; we did not hear it perhaps, or, if we did, we took little heed of it, yet it shot up arrow-like to heaven, and did a great work for us! We shall see when we get there what a power that blessing was, what it bought us, how supernaturally availing it has been to us; and we shall be much astonished ! These will be recognitions more joyful than the joyfullest meeting of a mother with her long-lost child on earth ; *il se fera alors des filiations éternelles, des liens d'un amour immortel entre les sauveurs et les sauvés.'*

The Archbishop went on in this strain, saying many beautiful and touching things which, unfortunately, I cannot recall ; even this much I should not have remembered accurately ; but that, on my return home, I noted down some of the remarks which had struck me most forcibly.

From speaking of the power of prayer in heaven, we came to talk of its efficacy on earth; I happened to remark how discouraging it was to our weak faith to see so many fervent prayers remain unanswered, notwithstanding our Divine Lord's pledge that whatever we asked in His name should be granted. The Archbishop denounced as false and unfilial the assertion that any fervent prayer ever did remain unanswered, and entered into a dissertation on prayer in itself, its nature, its office, its difficulties, its privileges, and the conditions essential to its acceptableness ; he spoke with great unction, and that persuasive eloquence that comes only from the heart.

'It is of faith,' he said, 'that no prayer made

in these dispositions can be unavailing; one very common impediment to our petitions being answered is, that we are always in a violent hurry, whereas God is slow in His ways; we turn off and say, He hasn't answered us, when literally we have not given Him time to answer. No, no, we have got a Father in heaven, and not a word is spoken, not a sigh is breathed from the hearts of one of His children on earth, but it straightway reaches Him; and nothing can reach Him and be sterile. The doctrine of the Communion of Saints teaches us that no particle of merit is ever lost in the treasury of the Church; the grace that is rejected by one, is offered to, and accepted by, another; like the seed that falls upon the rock, and is then wafted by the wind to some fertile spot, so the prayers that remain unproductive for the soul in whose immediate behalf they were sent up, are made over to another, where the soil is prepared by good desires, and whom they sanctify and save. Shall I tell you a little anecdote, *apropos* of this reversible action of prayer, which occurred to myself, and contributed more than any incident in my own experience to strengthen my faith in intercession?'

We assented, of course, with delight, and his Grace continued as follows :

'Soon after I had left the See of Nancy, which I had filled since 1859, I had occasion to revisit the diocese. During the one day that I spent there, many old friends flocked to see me. When I took my departure the next morning, Monsieur le Sénateur —— insisted on driving me in his gala carriage to the station, several of the notabilities followed after us in theirs, so that we made quite a little procession. At the station we found a crowd of good people waiting to wish their old shepherd *bon voyage*, and to get his blessing They opened a passage for me when I alighted, and I walked through their midst, blessing on either side of me uninterruptedly, when my attention was arrested by a little child struggling to push its way out to the front. I am fond of children, and make a point of going out of my way to bless them ; this was a tiny little maid, and she held out her hands, and looked up in my face with a timid eager expression, that drew my heart at once ; I stooped down, and laying my hand on her head, I blessed her, saying, " *Que ma bénédiction vous porte bonheur, mon enfant, à vous et aux votres !*" While I was pronouncing the words, and before I had withdrawn my hand, I saw an elderly lady, who was standing close behind the child, start, and utter what sounded like a suppressed cry of pain. My first thought was either that she had been suddenly seized with an acute physical pain, or that she was the mother of the little one, and labouring under some mental suffering to which the invocation, which I had spoken rather tenderly, adapted itself with peculiar fitness. I looked at her fixedly for a moment ; and laying my hand again on the fair little head that was still turned up to me, I repeated more emphatically than the first time, " *Que ma bénédiction vous porte bonheur, mon enfant, à vous et aux votres !*" The same suppressed exclamation broke from the lady, while the movement that accompanied it was more distinct and startling than before ; her features contracted ; and her whole body seemed convulsed by a sharp spasm of pain. There was no time to ask a question, or even to express a word of sympathy, for the bell was ringing, and I had just time to seat myself in the train when it moved on. The face and expression of that woman pursued me all the way to Paris ; next day, however, after making a memento for her during the Holy Sacrifice, I dismissed her from my mind, and thought no more of her. About a month later I again visited Nancy. On the evening of my arrival I was sitting with the Bishop, talking over matters concerning the administration of the diocese, when he said suddenly :

'O, I must not forget to mention something rather strange that has occurred lately, and which I connect with your last visit here.'

He then told me that, the day after I had left Nancy, a lady called at the Evêché and asked if I was expected there soon again ; on being told that I was not, she seemed distressed, so much so, that the porter suggested her seeing the Bishop, saying that he might be able to give her some information as to the probable time of my coming to the diocese, or else put her in communication with me, if Madame's business could be done by letter, &c. She hesitated for a moment ; but then shook her head, and walked away quickly, her countenance and manner betraying the greatest agitation. The porter was accustomed to see the door besieged by all classes and characters of visitors every day ; but there was something so odd about this one, so unlike the generality, that he took note of her, and mentioned the circumstance to the Bishop ; the lady, however, had left no clue as to who she was, or what she wanted, and his lordship could throw no light on the mystery. A week or so elapsed, and she again presented herself at the Palace, renewed her inquiries, and received the same answer as before. The porter again invited her to see the Bishop, who was just then at home, and would be happy to receive Madame, and could inform her more satisfactorily, and so on. This time she allowed herself to be persuaded, and had not to wait many minutes when the Bishop appeared. From him she learned that there was just a chance of my running up to Nancy in the course of the month; but I might not come till the end of the year. Her delight on hearing the first probability, and her despair when she came to the second, induced the Bishop to offer his services if it were in his power to replace me.

'Thank you,' she said; 'but you can do nothing for me. *Cet homme m'a troublée.* I wish I had never seen him! Perhaps it is better I should not see him again.'

She said this vehemently, but in an absent sort of way, as if she were thinking out some struggle that was going on in her mind; her manner was altogether so excited, that the Bishop, moved to compassion, urged her gently to confide in him, and unburden her heart of whatever was oppressing it. She thanked him less coldly than before, but replied that there was no use in her speaking to any one but Monseigneur Darboy ; and repeated again, '*Il m'a troublée cet homme, il m'a troublée.*' The Bishop fancied he saw in this eagerness on the one side, and obstinate reserve on the other, the work of divine grace goading her soul to some merciful result, in which either her own caprice, or some power that was controlling her mysteriously, had chosen me to be instrumental, so he suggested her coming to Paris to see me ; but she rejected that proposition in a tone that left no room for argument.

'It would be a fool's errand to go from Nancy to Paris to say nothing,' she replied, '*car en définitif je n'ai rien à lui dire !*'

'May I venture to put one question to you, Madame ? Are you a Christian ?' demanded the Bishop.

She looked at him defiantly.

'Well, and what if I be not ? All the more reason, perhaps, for my seeing Monseigneur Darboy !'

'Take my advice, Madame,' said the Bishop, 'don't wait for the visit of the Archbishop of Paris : go simply and pay a visit to the curé of your parish ; if you want consolation, he is a holy man, and well fitted to administer it ; if you are in need of instruction, he is a learned man, and competent to answer all your doubts and queries.'

She met this piece of advice with undisguised contempt ; but finally, after a good deal of persuasion, she agreed to go and see Monsieur le Curé, on the express condition that, as soon as ever I arrived at Nancy, she was to be sent for. She had kept her word, it seemed ; but nothing came of it beyond a certain loss of time and trial of patience to the curé, as the worthy man himself admitted to the Bishop, when the latter met him and made some inquiries as to his singular parishioner. His lordship now wished to make good his part of the bargain, and having put me in possession of the case, was about to despatch a messenger to the lady, when I cried : Hold ! My time was short, and I had a great deal to do ; if I saw this good lady I should, no doubt, have to hear her confession, and this would take up more time than I could at all spare ; moreover, my multifarious episcopal duties had obliged me, for some time past, to give up confessing women altogether, and there was nothing in this particular instance that I could see to justify my breaking through the rule. I could not take the Bishop's view of the case ; it appeared to me nothing more than an eccentric caprice, which I was neither bound nor inclined to encourage; he, however, was so eager, that I allowed myself to be overruled. A messenger was sent to inform Madame * * * that I would receive her at eleven o'clock the next morning.

The moment she entered the room, I recognised her as the stranger whose singular demeanour in the crowd had attracted my attention a month before. She was nervous and embarrassed, and evidently at a loss what to say to me. I broke the ice at once by alluding to our last meeting.

'When we met before, Madame,' I said, 'you were suffering either in mind or body; are you still in need of any help or comfort that I can give?'

She tried to speak, but could not articulate a word, and after a vain effort to control her emotion, she hid her face in her hands and completely broke down. I waited till she had recovered herself, and then asked her again to tell me the cause of her distress, and in what way I could serve her.

'Monseigneur,' she said, 'I hardly know myself what it is, or what I want of you, or what brought me here at all; ever since that day when you passed me on the platform I have been haunted day and night by the desire to see you again, and now that

I am satisfied I know not what to say to you. When I went with the crowd to see you pass, it was out of mere idle curiosity; I had no idea of asking for your blessing, I don't believe in such things, and when I saw the people fall on their knees before you, I thought what superstitious folly it was, and I knew there was a sneer of contempt on my face. I was afraid if you noticed me you would fancy I was there to get your blessing, and when you came near me and raised your hand I resented it as a mockery and an indignity, and I drew myself up as stiffly as I could that you might see it. You did not see me at first, but when you blessed that little child I felt as if some one had struck me a violent blow; the words you said went through me like a knife. I cannot describe the effect they produced in me, but it was one of acute physical pain, my whole body shook; this was repeated when you repeated the blessing, and the pain ceased when you ceased speaking; but the impression was so vivid that I had as it were a sense of it for days, in fact it has never left me. I have longed to see you and to speak to you, that you might give me back the peace which you took away from me, unconsciously no doubt; before that day I was calm and content, at peace with myself and with the world, but since then I have been tormented by a vague feeling of unrest; I cannot sleep; I cannot enjoy the things that have hitherto made life most interesting to me. I cannot say what has gone wrong; but the world altogether seems to have gone wrong. What can you do to set it right for me?'

Her manner, which was at the outset timid and deprecating, grew more emphatic as she proceeded, and she flung out the last sentence at me in a tone of defiance. The world had gone wrong with her, poor woman, and she challenged me to set it right. God was striving hard to do it for her, and she was kicking against Him with all her might. I was considering this, and turning it up and down in my mind how I should answer her, when she broke out with,

'I ought perhaps to tell you, Monseigneur, that I am a free-thinker; I have read the Gospel in the most impartial spirit, but all I could see in it is a beautiful legend, full of poetry and morality; it does not approve itself to me philosophically as divine, as bearing the impress of divine essential truth; in a word, I concluded that Christianity is a fable!'

She evidently expected this climax to elicit a

cry of horror from me. I was malicious enough to disappoint her, however, and remarked coolly,

'Après, Madame?'

'Après, Monseigneur,' she continued, ' I turned to the religion of nature and pure reason, and in it I found what I had vainly sought for elsewhere— peace and certainty. Voltaire, with his superhuman insight into the human heart, opened out to me, &c.'

In fact the wonders that Voltaire and his friends performed for the good lady were too great to be credited, if I could remember them all. She had read every book, it seemed to me, that had been written since Voltaire against religion and morality. Her childhood had had the blessings of a Christian home, but her parents both died when she was very young ; her mind, restless and inquisitive, had been poisoned by bad books, and her principles corrupted by the companionship of sceptics and infidels ; she had been married to an infidel before she was eighteen, and had been twenty years a widow ; her husband's death had embittered her, and closed her heart resentfully against God and all good influences ; she led me to understand, with a sort of defiant fearlessness, that since his death she had lived up to the standard of her miserable creed, worshipping pure nature, and seeking in her bereavement all the palliatives that nature unrestrained and unregenerated by grace holds out to suffering mortals. I let her go on till she had said all that was necessary to enlighten me on the state of her mind and guide me as to how I should deal with it; but then I stopped her; I had no notion of losing my time in a discussion on M. de Voltaire and pure reason, and I said so. She was very angry at this, for it was what she had been leading up to all along; the information she had volunteered about her antecedents and the history of her mind was simply a preliminary process towards clearing the ground for a fencing match, and when I peremptorily declined the performance altogether, she could not conceal her vexation and surprise. She was beginning a protest, but I interrupted her.

'Madame,' I said, 'you must excuse me; I have not the time for a controversy this morning, and if I had I should still decline it; it would be too unequal a match; you could not cope with me. Do not fancy I mean the least disrespect; but you overrate your knowledge. No doubt you are a very clever woman, and you have read more than most women, but you have read bad books, and read them in a bad spirit; of good books you have read very little, and too superficially to have profited even by that ; of theology you know nothing whatever, whereas my life from my boyhood up has been a sustained pursuit of that study. You see that it would be taking a shabby advantage of you if I engaged with you in a theological argument. No, I will not argue with you, but, if you wish it, I will instruct you ; but not here. I will go down to the church, and wait for you in the confessional ; there I can speak to you as one having authority, and with God's grace I will help you to a better peace than the false one you have lost.'

I stood up, and was moving towards the door, when she rose too, and cried out contemptuously :

'The confessional! I kneel down like a child, or a doating old *dévote*, in the confessional! I tell you I don't believe in the Gospel, and you ask me to go to confession ! You are mocking me, my lord !'

She tried to laugh, but her voice shook, and her mouth quivered, and told of the struggle that was going on within.

'Madame,' I said, and I tried to put into my tone and looks some of the pity that my heart was full of, ' it is you who are mocking God by resisting His grace ; you are not quite so unbelieving as you say, or else you would not be here now. God is very merciful, but take heed that you trifle not with

His mercy! Do as He commands you by the voice of His minister: follow me to the church.'

'I will never demean myself by such an act; I will never kneel down at the feet of a man!' she exclaimed passionately, and sat down again, as much as to say, 'Go your way without me; I will not stir!'

'I am going to the church,' I said, looking up at the clock, 'and I will wait there one hour.'

I went straight to the sacristy, where I put on a surplice and stole, and then entering the church I knelt down before the altar, and prayed with my whole heart for the poor soul over which God and the devil were, as it were, fighting hand to hand. I waited a long time—my eager watch made it seem much longer; the clock chimed the half-hour, and still I waited, and it must soon strike the hour, but no one came; my heart began to sink. God was being worsted in the duel. But just as I had given up all hope, I heard a door open softly at the other end of the church. I stood up at once, and without turning to see whether it was the person I expected, walked straight to the confessional. I had hardly closed the door when a quick step crossed the pavement, and the penitent was on her knees beside me. God had won the day!

T

Before I left Nancy I had the happiness of giving her Holy Communion, which she received in floods of tears, and in a spirit of joyful penitence that it has seldom been my privilege to witness. Her conversion was not the result of any passing emotion or over-wrought feeling; it proved as solid as it had been prompt. Madame * * * has persevered faithfully; her life is one of exemplary piety and active goodness; she works indefatigably for the curé of her parish, and with the docility of a child. It was a very happy visit of mine to Nancy, that one; and in recalling the many merciful episodes that have marked my ministry amongst souls, there is not one that I look back on with greater consolation.'

Monseigneur ceased speaking, and for some moments we remained all under the spell of his suppressed emotion, no one caring to break the silence. At last he said, brightening up with that merry twinkle in his eye that sometimes gave a sort of quizzical expression to his face:

'So you see what may come even of a blessing that one catches in the bustle of a railway station!'

This is all my story; but while the memory of Monseigneur Darboy's sufferings and death is still fresh in our minds, every little incident connected with his life is invested with a kind of sacred interest, and it will not be out of place here to record some conversation which I had with him on the occasion of our last meeting on earth.

It was on the 17th of August. Paris was seething with excitement. After alternating from mad jubilee to black despair, she had so far sobered down as to come to facts, and try to look at them and comprehend them. She began to see that she had been bamboozled and blindfolded; that the *soi-disantes* battles which France had won had never been fought; that the victories for which she had illuminated had never been won; that her arms, instead of being anywhere triumphant, were everywhere beaten; that she was reeling and staggering under the most appalling series of disasters history had yet chronicled; that it was no longer a question of 'kicking back the vandals across the Rhine,' but of saving themselves from utter annihilation; that the enemy was marching on the capital, and would soon be at its very gates: this was the reality to which poor, foolish, infatuated Paris was at last awaking. Still, even at this crisis, the general impression was that a siege was impossible; that it would take a million and a half of men to invest the city; that the Prussians were too exhausted in numbers to attempt such a gigantic enterprise; and that, admitting the nation, by a supreme effort, could muster the necessary forces, Bismarck would never dare, in the face of Europe and of history, commit his country to such a demoniacal act of vandalism as the bombardment of the noblest city in the world. Some who believed the unifier of Germany capable of bombarding heaven itself if his aims required it, and his artillery could range so high, consoled themselves by declaring that if the Prussians were mad enough to thrust themselves under the walls of Paris, every man of them, from first to last, should find his grave there: not a solitary woman's son of the million and a half should go back to tell the Vaterland how his brethren had perished! Vain vaunt of folly, and blindness, and ignorance, unparalleled in the history of men! But I did not mean to dwell on this; merely to glance at it on my way to the Archbishop, whom we went to consult, on this 17th of August, as to the prudence of remaining in Paris or flying to England. Most of our countrymen had already adopted the latter alternative, and the few who still lingered on, had packed their trunks, and got their passports *visés*, and were ready to start at an hour's warning. His Grace unhesitatingly advised us to follow their example.

'But, Monseigneur,' I said, 'you don't believe in the city being besieged? Surely, in the 19th century, such a thing is beyond the pale of possibility?' and the idea seemed so absurd that I laughed as I spoke.

But the Archbishop looked very grave.

'We may hope it will not come to that,' he said; 'but we must act as if we were certain it would.'

'And you, Monseigneur,' I ventured to ask, 'what will you do?'

'Stay where I am, of course!' he answered gaily. 'Thank God, I have not to puzzle over my duty; it is ready marked out for me, and I shall have plenty of work to do!'

'It is a fearful day of judgment that has overtaken the world,' I said; 'and one dares not think how it will end. What will become of France, for instance, if the Emperor is killed? Who is there to take his place?'

'*Ah, voilà!*' he exclaimed, lifting his arm and letting it fall again heavily on the arm of his *fauteuil*, 'that is the terrible consequence of having all depend on the life of one; we can forecast nothing; we are at the mercy of the first adventurer who may start up and seize the helm; *quel sera cet homme de courage, ou de crime?*'

He said a good deal on the same subject, speaking with a calm foreboding that had much prophetic instinct in it; but the mighty questions which the coming shadows of events evolved in all thinking minds during those momentous days have been in some measure answered since, and there is no need to ponder now in the retrospect on Monseigneur Darboy's previsions. That those previsions did not date from the crisis of to-day is evident enough, from the Pastorals in which, of late years, the Archbishop had daringly denounced the vices and follies of the Empire, and foretold their inevitable culmination. Again and again he had raised his voice in solemn warning to the leaders and the people. In his Pastoral of 1865 occurs the following passage, which we cannot read now without being struck by the clear-sighted intelligence of the statesman and the far-sighted wisdom of the prophet stamped on every line: 'Yes, when immoral and irreligious doctrines have warped the intellect and corrupted the heart of the nation, when license and luxury have overrun society, when all manner of fictitious wants have been introduced into every class, when all this has been accomplished, there will come the day of reckoning ; then we shall see the intelligence of the great disturbed, the prudence of the wise will grow short, their strength will be hindered, and it will need but one of those thousand accidents that swarm in the existence of peoples to precipitate *all* into the abyss, and make established institutions collapse *dans un suprême écroulement.*'

Some remark on the convulsed state of France, and the European complications likely to ensue, led to the mention of Rome. A great deal of gossip, written and spoken, had been circulated all over the world concerning the light in which the Archbishop of Paris stood towards the Holy See, and the attitude he had maintained during the Council ; rumour had been very busy, and, as usual, very inaccurate in her appreciation of both ; a great deal of scandal had been given and taken on the score of his supposed opposition to the dogma of Infallibility, and I felt a strong desire to hear from his own lips the truth on this vexed point. The confidence with which he had always encouraged me to speak to him, and the simplicity with which he condescended to explain his own views on other subjects, prompted me to ask him for a few words of explanation on this one. I felt, too, that we were likely to adopt his advice and leave Paris in a day or two, and that another such favourable opportunity of putting the request might not occur again. This would probably be our last interview for a long time; I little guessed how long! I therefore asked him boldly if he would give us his version of the controversy, which had engaged many holy and learned men, with regard to Papal Infallibility.

'*Très volontiers!*' he replied, with alacrity; 'my own share of it can be stated in a few words: we went to Rome to consult together, not on the promulgation of a dogma, as so many people both inside and outside the Church were ignorant enough to suppose, but on the definition of a dogma which has always existed; I, with some others, considered this definition inadequately framed, and as I had been summoned to give my opinion, I gave it without fear or reticence. The definition stood thus:* The Pope is infallible when, inspired by God, he pronounces on any question of theology or morality. I was for inserting the clause: *et appuyé par les*

---

* Though I wrote down this conversation the day after it took place, I may have made mistakes in the exact expressions; but I trust that the meaning and spirit of the Archbishop's remarks will be clear to my Catholic readers.

moyens d'inspiration reconnus dans l'Eglise (and supported by the means of inspiration recognised in the Church). This was rejected on the grounds that it was so palpably self-evident to Catholics, having been taught and understood by all generations from St. Peter down, that to insert it would be idle tautology and a pandering to the indocile spirit of the age. The Holy Father took this view of the case. The Council adopted it, and we all of us, *moi le premier*, accepted its decision, and made an end of controversy. We know that the voice of the Church is the voice of God; that her decrees are infallibly dictated by the Spirit of God; and all we have to do, as good sons, is to obey her and to uphold her teaching to our utmost by word and deed.'

It is with heartfelt pleasure and deep gratitude that I record these words. The accent of earnest conviction with which they were spoken, I cannot record; there was that in the tone and look of the Archbishop as he uttered them that made you feel he was speaking from the abundance of the heart, not from any compulsory sense of duty, as one would who, *nolens volens*, succumbs to a fiat imposed by his conscience but resented by his reason. I remembered the story told somewhere of an infidel who, on coming out from a sermon of Monseigneur Darboy's, exclaimed, 'I am not a Christian; but if I were to hear that man often, I should soon be one in spite of myself.'

There was some further conversation about the Council, and the state of feeling in Rome while it lasted; the ladies, it was remarked, had contributed in no small degree to keep up the thermometer of theological excitement in society, holding *salons faillibilistes* and *salons infaillibilistes*, arguing and discussing and criticising the Fathers, their speeches, their merits, demeanour, &c.; and altogether expending their energies, better employed elsewhere, on what they knew nothing at all about. *Apropos* of this, some one repeated a *mot* of Monseigneur P——'s. One of these crinoline theologians met the Bishop one evening at a sister *faillibiliste's*, and told him that some one had named her and her co-doctoresses '*les mères du Concile;*' '*Les commères,** Madame,*' replied Monseigneur, with a profound bow, and passed on. Monseigneur Darboy laughed heartily at the story, and said it was a great pity people had not prayed more and talked less on the subject, as they might thereby have done some good and avoided much evil.

* Gossips.

I cannot close this reminiscence better than by quoting the opening lines of his own will, dated September 16, 1870, the eve of the investment of Paris: '*I die in the faith of the Holy Church Catholic, Apostolic, and Roman, believing all that she believes, condemning all that she condemns.*'

He blessed us all when we took leave of him, and prayed that we might meet in happier times. When that prayer is granted, it must be in the sunshine of the Father's house, where the martyr is resting now; and we may find that the blessing which he called down on us that day will have helped us to rejoin him there.

Martyr! But is he a martyr? I hear you exclaim; not enviously, perhaps; not grudging God the glory, or George Darboy the joy of having added one more victor to the ranks of those who have shed their blood for Christ, and now stand before the throne 'clad in crimson,' and holding in their hand the palm-branch; you are afraid only of bestowing the title where it is not due. You need not be afraid. It was fairly and nobly won. The Archbishop of Paris was no mere political victim, as many would make him out; he was not persecuted to death because he was Cæsar's friend, and because he represented a name and a system odious to the Commune, but because he symbolised Him whose name was more odious and far more formidable to those mad fanatics than all the kings and powers of this world combined; because he was the minister of God—'*le serviteur d'un nommé Dieu*,' as they blasphemously put it elsewhere—the first representative of religion in Paris.

The story of Monseigneur Darboy's captivity and death has been told many times, but it has generally been either mutilated or embellished; in no instance that I know of has it been told by any one who was an eye-witness from the beginning; the greater part of what was written about it at the time was the result either of conjecture or invention. The following details were given me by one who is qualified to speak with certainty of the events of those terrible days, having been arrested at the same time as the Archbishop, and, after sharing his captivity, witnessing—more closely, at least, than any other person we know of—his death. They reveal no startling episodes, and are quite bare of melodramatic colouring; but they are strictly and exhaustively true, and therefore cannot fail to interest those who knew the Archbishop, and all those who care to know how that brave and gentle champion of Christ met Death, and bore himself while awaiting it.

Hints came from many quarters that the Archbishop was going to be arrested. My informant—whose name, for private reasons, I am requested to suppress—was told that the warrant was already made out, and might be presented at any moment. He went to Monseigneur Darboy, and implored him to seek safety in flight while there was yet time; many others joined their entreaties to the same end, urging every possible argument to induce him to fly, but Monseigneur resolutely refused to do so.

'My duty is here,' he answered calmly, repeating almost the same words he had used nine months before to me: 'I will remain at my post till they drive me from it.'

'But think of others, Monseigneur; you will not be driven alone; we shall all be seized with you!' said one of his secretaries.

'I think not,' replied the Archbishop; 'I think they will be satisfied when they have got the chief. When they come, I will just say to them, "Here I am; take me, and let these go their way."'

He would fain have induced others to adopt the advice they gave, and counselled any of his immediate clergy to save themselves by flight, and leave him to meet the danger alone; but this trait of resemblance with his Master was denied the Archbishop; they indignantly refused to desert their shepherd, and, braver than the unconfirmed Apostles, one and all stood by him to the last.

Let it not be supposed that it was from want of realising the situation, that Monseigneur Darboy awaited it so calmly. He realised it from the first; more clearly than any one around him he foresaw what was coming. On the 20th of March, two days after the saturnalia of the 18th, which the limp *bourgeoisie* of Paris chose to laugh at, declaring that it would 'die of its own ridicule' before the Party of Order were driven to interfere, the Père Perraud tells us that the Archbishop startled him by observing with calm gravity, 'Things will go on like this for a few days, *and then they will grow worse.*'

Meantime he went his way as if nothing had broken the smooth current of his daily life. No one would have thought, to see the bright alacrity with which he went through his round of duties, that anything was amiss or changed in the world outside. His cheerfulness never deserted him; he seemed to think only of doing his duties, each as it came to his hand, cheating those around him into comparative forgetfulness of danger, so entirely did he ignore it himself.

But the sword fell at last. On the 4th of April, between four and five in the afternoon, the gens-d'armes of the Commune broke into his presence in the old Palace of the Rue de Grenelle, and presented their ' *mandat d'arrêt* against the person of George Darboy, calling himself Archbishop of Paris.' They offered no violence, nor used any offensive language beyond that contained in their warrant; they assured the prisoner that he might consider himself solely in the light of a hostage, and fear nothing at the hands of the Commune; he would be treated with every consideration, and allowed all the privileges consistent with his safe keeping. The Archbishop believed these plausible protestations so fully that, when one of his secretaries went to take leave of him at the carriage-door, his Grace said,

'Perhaps I shall send for you this evening; tell my valet, too, to be ready to come to me: I may want him.'

He was allowed to drive to the Conciergerie in his own carriage, which happened to be waiting in the courtyard. On arriving at the prison, however, the tone of the Commune changed. The venerable prelate was subjected to what my informant described as *un examen ignoble*. Raoul Rigault, who headed the commission, said to him in an insulting tone, accompanied by a threatening gesture,

'Ah, we have you now—you who have been the masters these 1800 years! Our turn has come; but we shall treat you better than you treated us. Instead of burning you, we shall content ourselves with shooting you.'

This was admitting clearly enough that it was not at the Senator, or the Grand Almoner of the Empire, that their vengeance was pointed, but at the minister of a religion which, for 1800 years, had warred against the principles, and foiled the efforts, of that portion of humanity represented by Raoul Rigault and his colleagues.

No sooner were the Archbishop and his staff out of the Archiepiscopal Palace than the Freemasons bore down upon it, and established themselves in the various rooms, sixty of them remaining there till the fall of the Commune. Over the door of the Secretariat they inscribed the words: *Secretariat de la Franc-maçonnerie;* the inscription is still visible, or was a few days ago.* The chapel

* This sketch was written in May 1871, immediately after the defeat of the Communists by the Versailles troops.

they turned into a banquet-hall, and the walls which had echoed to the tinkle of the Mass bell and the song of prayer and worship, now witnessed orgies that no Christian pen may dwell upon.

'If you want a parallel to the scenes enacted there by the Freemasons,' said my informant, 'open the Bible, and to the feast of Belshazzar superadd every sacrilegious profanity that modern cynicism can devise, and you will have some idea of the reality.'

Nor did the merry-makers mean to stop at this. They had taken measures for the total destruction of the building by fire, and were only prevented by want of time from carrying out the plan. At the last, when the approach of Versailles became known, there was a general *sauve-qui-peut*, and in the hurry and terror and confusion of flight everything but their own personal safety seemed to have been forgotten. Three large cases of inflammable bombs, a quantity of powder and petroleum, and other combustible material, were found in the rooms of one of the secretaries, M. l'Abbé Petit. This gentleman was not arrested with Monseigneur Darboy, as it has been stated, but late the same night; he knew there was a warrant out for his apprehension, and he was surprised they did not seize him at once;

but he felt certain they would do so before long. He retired to rest at his usual hour, but he could not sleep; a presentiment of coming evil kept him wakeful; and when at midnight he heard a sound of arms clanking in the *salon* next his bedroom, he was startled, but not surprised to see the *gens de la Commune* enter boisterously and bid him get up and come with them. Another escort roused Mademoiselle Darboy, the sister of the Archbishop, who was staying in the house at the time, and hurried her off to the Conciergerie. They allowed her maid to accompany her, and she was permitted, I believe, to have her food supplied from without; many of the hostages were, in the beginning. The Commune was either very capricious in its treatment to the same class of offenders, or the jailers, in executing their orders, were amenable to a certain obvious argument, which seldom fails to carry conviction to their minds; at any rate, some of the captives were permitted to buy off a good deal of material misery and discomfort, and to get clean clothes and good food, while to others, charged with no greater offences, these luxuries were inexorably denied.

Some were allowed to receive letters and visits, while their next-door captives, for no reason then or now ostensible, were kept in complete isolation.

My informant, for instance, who was condemned *au grand secret*, and rigorously shut away from any communication, direct or indirect, with the world outside, was nevertheless able to get his food brought daily from his own house, and to have clean linen regularly supplied to him; the greatest precaution was taken to prevent his making use of either of these mediums to send or receive messages, but he contrived to elude the lynx eyes of his guardians, who scrupulously examined every dish and every article of clothing that entered and left his cell. One day, as he was cutting an omelet, he felt the spoon stopped by something thick and tough; with the quick instinct of a captive it flashed upon him that the impediment was a message of some sort; he managed to withdraw it and hide it without being observed, and as soon as he was alone, proceeded to examine the half-melted greasy little roll of paper. His faithful *bonne* had hit upon this means of asking him to let her know if there was anything she could do to help him, or if he had any commands that she could execute for him; she suggested his answering her in the hem of one of his stockings. The prisoner adopted the hint, taking the precaution to damp the stocking and crumple the paper well before he slipped it into the hiding-place. Through this somewhat irregular vehicle he managed to send out his last will and testament, which the good soul placed in safe keeping, and had the joy of handing back to her master when he was restored to freedom.

As a proof of the terrible effect of solitary confinement on a human being, I may mention here what he told me of its effect upon himself. He said that when, after many weeks of solitude, the turnkey came to open his door and lead him out as he believed to be shot there and then, he quite forgot the horror of the crisis in his joy at the prospect of seeing his fellow-creatures once more, and hearing their voices even for a moment; the torturing suspense, the weary, tomb-like silence of the preceding weeks had brought him to the verge of madness, and he would have welcomed death as a glad and merciful release. How or why he escaped the fate of his companions he cannot say. It would seem that after the murder of the Archbishop, all minor acts of vengeance were forgotten, and many victims who stood daily awaiting the great Deliverer were abandoned in their cells, where they might have starved to death if the soldiers of Versailles had not come in time to set them free.

Monseigneur Darboy only remained two days at

the Conciergerie, whence he was transported to Mazas. The circumstances of his life there have been made known to us by those visitors who were allowed access to him from time to time in the earlier days. The accommodation was of the most miserable description, a cell like any common prisoner's, thief or forger. The Archbishop was permitted to supply his own food from a restaurant, and he received letters and papers, and occasionally, by a special pass from the Commune, visits. But any privilege granted to him in the day was amply paid for at night. The Federals, emulating from the first the cruelty of the jailer Simon to Louis XVII., were accustomed to amuse themselves during the tedious night-watches by knocking at the door of the Archbishop, and waking him suddenly out of his tired sleep with oaths and insults, bidding him get ready to come out and be shot. One of the turnkeys at Mazas, who had been a constant eye-witness to this cruel joke, told the Père Perraud that the victim bore it invariably in uncomplaining silence, and never once showed the slightest sign of impatience towards his tormentors. The deep peace of the martyr's spirit was beyond the reach alike of insult and resentment. He was looking calmly to the end, awaiting it, not alone with resignation, but with impatient longing. When a friend, who had gained access to his cell, was describing the aspect of Paris, cut up by barricades that were bristling with cannon, the Archbishop cried out impulsively,

'O, how I envy Monseigneur Affre! would that like him I could have ascended a barricade, and died there!'

But a great joy awaited the hostages, one which was to take the sting out of all their sufferings, and give them strength to endure to the end. A noble woman, whose name I long to give but may not, devised a stratagem for conveying the Blessed Sacrament to one of the Jesuit Fathers, and executed it at the peril of her own life. You have seen those conical tin cans, called *boîtes-au-lait*, in the dairy windows in Paris? She had one of these made with a false bottom, in which twenty-five consecrated Hosts were concealed, and thus surreptitiously passed into the prison; she managed at the same time and by the same agency, to send the Père a number of tiny flax cases to be used as pyxes, in which the prisoners could keep the Blessed Sacrament.

Who will tell us of the transports of love and thanksgiving with which these heroic souls received the precious gift and carried it on their breasts?

With what living faith they must have broken the Bread of Life unto themselves, waiting in calm triumph for the moment when they might consume the last particle as their viaticum ! How deep and tender must have been their uninterrupted communion with the Divine Guest, whose Eucharistic Presence was more welcome to them in their captivity than the manna to the hungry Israelites in the desert! We get some faint idea of it from that Alleluia that breaks forth like a heavenly canticle from the pen of Père Clerc, writing to announce the glad tidings: 'All arrived in perfect condition, and everything was arranged with admirable tact and diligence. There is no more prison, no more solitude.... Ah, my Lord and my God, how kind Thou art! How true it is that the compassion of Thy Sacred Heart will never be belied! I could never have dared to conceive even the hope of such a favour; to possess our Lord, to have Him as the companion of my captivity, to carry Him on my heart, and to repose on His as He permitted His own beloved John to do! O, it is too much ;... the very thought of it overpowers me. And yet it is true. . . . . . O prison, dear prison, whose walls I have burst, exclaiming " *Bona Crux !*" what a happiness I owe thee! You are no longer a prison.

You are a shrine. You are not even a solitude to me, since I am no longer alone, but have my Saviour and my King dwelling with me. O, last for ever, dear prison, since you have gained me the joy of carrying my Lord on my heart, not as a symbol, but as the realisation of my union with Him. I always hoped that God would grant me the strength to die well; but this day my hope is changed into a true and solid confidence. I may now dare to say that I can do all things in Him who strengthens me, and who accompanies me to death. Will He indeed so will it? I know not; but this I know, that if He will it not, my regret will be for ever inconsolable.'

Brave son of St. Ignatius! God will spare you this regret.

On Monday evening, the 21st of May, an order came for the hostages to be removed from Mazas to La Roquette. This was understood to be the beginning of the end; it was welcomed exultingly by some, bravely by all. The hostages were collected in the courtyard, where they were waiting for several minutes before the Archbishop made his appearance. At first sight they could hardly believe it was indeed he; he was wan and emaciated as a skeleton; his beard had been allowed to grow during his confinement, and hung white and ragged and unkempt upon his breast, and he was so feeble as to seem scarcely able to support himself. One of his own secretaries did not recognise him, till Monseigneur Darboy, as soon as he espied him, exclaimed in surprise,

'Ah, so you too are here, *mon ami !*' and held out his hand.

The priest fell upon his knees and kissed it, that venerable hand that was soon to be uplifted to call down, with his last breath, a blessing on his murderers.

'You are ill, Monseigneur; you are suffering,' said the Abbé.

'Yes, I have suffered a good deal here,' replied the Archbishop, putting his hand to his side; 'I put a blister on it some days ago, and it is very painful.'

Père Olivaint went up to speak to him; and, in answer to some question of the Père's, Monseigneur said, '*I am dying of hunger !*'

Père Olivaint at once drew from his pocket a little tin box, in which there was one remaining pastille of chocolate, and gave it to him; he ate it, and, little as it was, it seemed to revive him.

They set out to La Roquette. The hostages were not taken in the ordinary van of the condemned; it was not large enough; they were huddled *pêle-mêle* into a sort of *déménagement* wagon, open at both ends. Monsieur Bonjean was beside the Archbishop; by his courage and Christian piety, the aged President edified them all, and proved himself worthy of his place in that grand and goodly company.

The journey lasted over three-quarters of an hour. All along the road, from prison to prison, the victims were mocked and hooted by the multitude; women, young girls, and children conspicuous in the demoniacal hubbub, gesticulating like drunken furies, throwing their caps and aprons into the air, waving red handkerchiefs, and shaking their clenched fists at the van, and shouting, '*A bas les rabats! A mort les prêtres! Qu'on les égorge! Qu'on les assassine! Qu'on en finisse!*' and other cries which may not be repeated here. One of the priests wore his *rabat;* the mob seemed particularly exasperated by the sight of it, and kept pointing at it, hissing and spitting all the while. Monsieur Bonjean thought it would stop the cursing and quiet them a little if the obnoxious symbol disappeared, so he said to the Abbé,

'Put your handkerchief round your neck, *mon Père.*'

The Abbé did so, but it failed to propitiate them; the yells and threats continued with unabated fury to the end.

At last the van stopped at La Roquette, and passed with its freight another step heavenward under the Gate of the Condemned. The hostages alighted in the *préau;* they were kept waiting there one hour and a half before they were taken to their cells. During this delay many of them confessed one to another, either standing together as if engaged in ordinary conversation, or walking up and down, muttering their confessions in short sentences, stopping every now and then, and looking indifferently about them, while the words of absolution were being pronounced by each upon the other: for the jailers were watching them, ready at the first suspicious sympton to pounce on the penitents like tigers on their prey.

One of the priests, the one from whom I hold these details, had not been able to snatch a moment alone with any of his brethren, owing to two of the guards standing close by him; so when the signal was given for them to be on the move to their cells, he said to a turnkey,

'Lock me in with one of my comrades, so that we may be able to chat a little; do, like a good fellow!'

But the man turned on him savagely, and said, '*Taisez-vous, Soutane!*' and pushed him aside.

They were called out separately by their names, and locked up. The cells at La Roquette were originally large ones; each is now divided into two by a lath-and-plaster partition that cuts the window in twain, but without going close up to it; there is just space enough between to pass your hand through. There is not a stick of furniture in the cells, nothing but a straw palliasse and one blanket, both in a state of filth too loathsome to be described.

In Monseigneur Darboy's cell, whether by accident or by special concession to his rank, there was an old straw chair without a back, also a wooden plank in guise of a table. The day after his arrival some fresh straw and a comparatively clean blanket were brought to him; but he never used them; before night came the frail worn-out body was resting on another bed.

Let us borrow here a page from the Rév. Père de Pontlevoy's touching narrative :*

'The first recreation took place from eight to nine o'clock, when the people of the prison cleaned

---

* *Actes de la Captivité et de la Mort des cinq Pères de la Compagnie de Jésus*, p. 130.

out the poor cells. The universal character of these intervals of relaxation and reunion was the serenity of intimate communion; hearts are drawn towards each other much more quickly in community of faith and trial; old acquaintances were renewed, new ones were formed; all eagerly exchanged consolations; above all, they confessed to one another. ... Père Olivaint seemed to attach himself specially to the person of the Archbishop of Paris. Sometimes the suffering prelate, exhausted by privations and pain, remained stretched on his miserable bed; while Père Olivaint, seated at his feet, talked with him over the present and past. Could they yet speak of the future? From the first days of their arrival at La Roquette the bread even was scarce. The battle raging in the streets, and which was hourly gaining ground, interrupted probably the regular supplies of the prison. Père Olivaint drew on the slender provisions that yet remained to him, and brought the sinking pontiff a little gingerbread and a few cakes of chocolate. Thus was it given to a poor religious to exercise charity towards an Archbishop of Paris.'

My informant was put into the cell next to Père Caubert. They soon discovered the slit between the window and the wall, and great was their delight at the opportunity of conversing which it afforded them.

The Père asked his companion if he had the Blessed Sacrament about him; the other, surprised at the question, replied that he had not, upon which Père Caubert passed him a pyx containing an entire Host. My poor friend could hardly believe his eyes; and was so overpowered with joy, that he could only thank him by a flood of tears. The Father then told him how, and through whose intervention, the precious gift had found its way to them; they talked for some time of their separate experiences in the common captivity, and spent the remainder of the evening in prayer and reciting the divine office.

The hours dragged on with a kind of supernatural slowness. They knew they were to be shot that evening; but they had no idea at what hour, so that every step that sounded along the stone corridor, every key that grated in a door, made their hearts leap with a new thrill of awful expectation; but the night came and went, and still they were waiting. For some reason the programme was changed. Tuesday passed in the same suspense.

At last, on Wednesday evening, the 24th of

May, at half-past seven, the Director of the prison, a ruffian named Lefrançais, who had graduated for the sinister celebrity of this day's work by six years' hard labour at the galleys, ascended the stair leading to the condemned cells; he was accompanied by fifty Federal soldiers. They ranged themselves silently on the side of the gallery opposite the cells, and Lefrançais summoned the condemned aloud:

'Darboy!'
'Allard!'
'Bonjean!'
'Duguerry!'
'Clerc!'
'Ducoudray!'

A brigadier opened the corresponding cell-door, and the prisoner came forth and answered, '*Présent!*'

All else was hushed as death. There was no hurry or excitement, but something appalling in the cold-blooded quiet that reigned from first to last. Not a sound was heard but the rough voice of the convict, and the retreating steps of the prisoners as one by one they passed down to the courtyard.

Let me describe the outline of La Roquette; it will help you to realise the scene. The building itself stands, like most French prisons, in the centre of a vast court called the *préau;* this is enclosed by a thick stone wall, outside which is a space called the *Chemin de Ronde*, enclosed by another wall of the same height and depth as the first; this outer wall opens on the Rue Folie-Regnault, beyond which lies a large piece of waste ground. The prisoners, when they are allowed exercise, take it on the *préau;* they never pass the inner wall except on their way to execution.

It had been first arranged that the Archbishop and his companions were to be shot in the *préau;* and they were kept waiting there several minutes before the order was reversed; then they were taken out into the *Chemin de Ronde*.

The cells which they had just left give on the *préau*, so my informant had a full view of the procession which passed close under his window on its way to the *Chemin de Ronde*.

Père Allard walked first, with a soldier on either side of him; next came the Archbishop, leaning on Monsieur Bonjean; he looked more wan and shrunk than on the Monday before, and so feeble that he seemed with difficulty to support himself; but his countenance was very serene, and he raised his hand several times to bless as he went along. My friend could not say in what order the others followed. 'I saw only Monseigneur,' he said, 'I looked at no one else; and as soon as he disappeared through the gate of the *préau*, I fell upon my knees and began to recite aloud the Litany for the Dying. Père Caubert gave the responses; but before we had finished it, the rattle of the musketry drowned our voices.'

I was particularly anxious to know if Monseigneur Darboy had really uttered those words about 'dying for Faith and Liberty' which the accounts of the day attributed to him; but as far as my friend could judge, there is no authority whatever for the statement. He himself rejects it; and from what I knew of the Archbishop, I feel inclined to do so too. There was nothing melodramatic about him at any time; he was genuinely and consistently simple, the last man in the world to avail himself of a tragic opportunity, of closing his sacrifice with one of those stately or pregnant *mots* which his countrymen in particular have often thought it becoming to bequeath to posterity from the foot of the scaffold, as a legacy of wisdom or wit. I think we may safely dismiss as apocryphal the speech about Faith and Liberty, and consign it to the list of sensational phrases falsely attributed to great men under the same solemn circumstances. In the first place, if the wretches who fired on him were brutal enough to taunt him at such a moment with coarse and bitter words for his antagonism to what they and their leaders called liberty, and his life-long efforts to restrain it, Monseigneur Darboy was not assuredly in a mood to be spurred to any word of indignant retort; his spirit was too much absorbed in recollection of the August Presence into which he was about to enter. On the other hand his body was so worn and weak that, humanly speaking, he could not have pitched his voice high enough to have been heard by any one but the person standing close to him; it seemed as if it were only by a superhuman effort of will that he was able to drag himself to the place of execution. It is most improbable, therefore, that he spoke at all, unless it were, indeed, by a last act of sublime charity in imitation of his Divine Master, to call down a blessing on his murderers.

The story of the two soldiers having fallen on their knees, and implored his forgiveness for the crime they were forced to perpetrate, must also remain conjectural.* We would wish it to be true, and we may think it is, but as yet no eye-witness

* The subsequent trials left this incident in the same doubt.

has come forward to testify to its truth or falsehood.

That Monseigneur Darboy raised his hand to bless, simultaneously with the word of command which silenced his voice for ever, is most likely; the simple discharge of duty to the last, embodied in that gentle act of mercy, is in sweet harmony with his character and his life; moreover the mutilated right hand with the thumb and index cut clear off seem palpable evidence of the fact.

The appearance of the remains when they were conveyed from the *fosse commune* to the Rue de Grenelle so many days after, attested that death had been instantaneous; notwithstanding the revolting manner of the burial, flung as the victims were *en masse* into a shallow pit, their blood mixing with the slush and mud that oozed down on all sides from the banks of upturned clay, the Archbishop's features were distinctly recognisable. His heart was pierced through by two chassepôt bullets, and from this wound the life-blood had poured swiftly and copiously.

In retracing the earlier steps of Monseigneur Darboy's career, we are struck by certain coincidences that assume now the character of something like supernatural presentiments. His first sermon, preached in his native parish of Fayl-Billot two months before his ordination, had for its subject the happiness of the martyrs and the glory of suffering persecution and death for Christ's sake. The eloquence which the young deacon displayed on the occasion called forth enthusiastic predictions as to his future fame and advancement; but the little world who witnessed this first flight of sacred oratory descried in it nothing more; no one saw in the choice of his theme a promise; no one suspected that the joys which the ardent young priest painted in such glowing colours were one day to be his own portion, that five-and-thirty years hence he would be called upon to emulate the faithful patient heroism of the martyrs which to-day, on the threshold of his brilliant career, he dwelt upon so lovingly, with such envy and admiration. This enthusiasm for the glory of martyrdom never forsook him. He could never speak of earthly glory without being as it were irresistibly carried away to contrast the phantom that men call by that name with the true glory of the Christian, which in his beautiful commentaries on the *Imitation* he defines as 'the privilege of completing in our selves, by suffering, the mystery of our Redemption.'

In 1841, at the age of eight-and-twenty, when

professor at the Grand Seminary of Langres, the Abbé Darboy wrote some remarkable pages entitled *The Apathy of Good People*, in which he denounces with great vigour and with a maturity of style and thought surprising in so young a writer, the attitude of those *gens de bien* in France, who stood by shaking their heads and moralising over the ruin of their country when they ought to have been up and in the thick of action. 'Ah,' he cries, 'when the monarchy is overthrown, future races passing near the ruins will ask what the last Frenchmen did to postpone the supreme crisis; and history will answer: They looked on with their arms crossed; not a thrill of active indignation, of sublime courage, caused those cowardly and degenerate hearts to beat....' Then pointing with prophetic finger to the inevitable decay of faith in the nation as the result of its apathy, and to the hatred and persecution of God and His Church, which was certain to be the consequence of this decay, he closes his address by these memorable words: 'When, therefore, they shall come and ask me for my head in the name of Jesus Christ, I hope in the mercy of God to give me courage to present it with my hands clasped, and praying for my executioners as my elders did fifty years ago.'

In his preface to the Life of St. Thomas of Canterbury, a work pronounced by divines a masterpiece of theological and historical lore, the Abbé Darboy, touching on the same chord, says: 'Man borrows his true glory from the principles which he represents and from the courage with which he professes and defends them. Happy the man who enrols himself under the flag of a noble cause, and who knows how to live and, if needs be, to die for it!... Yes, to suffer and die for having loved the Church, is a destiny to be desired, beautiful and useful above all others!'

When in recognition of the service he had rendered to the Church and the faithful, by this Life of St. Thomas, he was presented with the Pectoral Cross of the English martyr, the Abbé Darboy held the precious relic in his hand for a moment, and then replied, '*J'en accepte l'augure, comme archevêque et comme martyre.*'

He was called to the See of Paris in 1863, and in his first Pastoral, written after taking possession of it, he says, alluding to the stormy times in which he had come to that post of eminence and danger, 'I am ready to give my life for the Church.' God took him at his word. He held the exalted and difficult charge of the archbishopric like one who is 'passing through,' who may not tarry on the road; like a steward and a pilgrim, vigilant and detached, ready at an hour's notice to lay down his honours and deliver up his trust, bearing out truly in spirit and in deed those words which he had written years before: 'Let us not give up our hearts to the fascination of earthly joys and goods, but let us pass through their midst like men who are going higher and further.' When all the honours of the Church and State were gathered upon his head, George Darboy remained unaltered by the perilous burden, carrying it like a garment that might at any moment slip from his shoulders. He retained under the mitre of St. Denis the simple grace which had characterised his bearing and manners as a seminarist, easy of access to all, devoid of hauteur, yet exercising nevertheless that sway of episcopal supremacy, which made one of his clergy observe, after having been admitted for the first time to the Archbishop's presence: 'He was as simple as a village curé, yet nobody ever before inspired me with so much awe.'

One more quotation from his own pen and I have done. It is from his Advent Pastoral of 1870. Paris was writhing in the throes of hunger and perishing with cold; her fortitude needed to be sustained. The Archbishop first struck the note of patriotism, and adjured his flock by every human motive to bear up bravely, to endure yet a little while, and leave their name and their example a monument of noble citizenship to France and to the world unto the end of time; and then, pointing beyond the thin partition of time to the great goal of eternity, he exclaimed: 'Let us stand at our post, and do our duty like good soldiers, under the eye of our true and sovereign Chief, and when death comes it will find us ready; its summons will be to us an awakening from sleep, the vanishing of a dream, the dawn of the real day, and of the life which is the beginning of bliss!'

Faithful to his own duty, he stood by it to the last; when he could do no more, he died for it.

And now that the red tide has ebbed away, what traces has it left behind, what signs do we gather of its passage? Will it prove, like the blood of the martyrs to old Rome, a power to cleanse and fertilise, to plant and bring forth from its death-wave fruits unto life and immortality; or has it been only the destroying torrent of the lava sweeping all before it into ruin and chaos and desolation, leaving as its trophies tombs and remorse and the dry bones of its victims? Whitherward did it travel, that blood-red tide? Down into the abyss whence nought comes up but smoke of darkness and vapours of hate? Or has it broken like a strong regenerating wave upon the breast of France, and sunk into her heart, and shall we see it lift itself up to heaven in white clouds of sorrow that will break and deluge her people in the saving flood of penitential tears? May it be so! May the blood of her martyred priests plead for France with the divine omnipotence of sacrifice, and cry out with a mighty voice for mercy on the stricken land!

THE END.

www.ingramcontent.com/pod-product-compliance
Lightning Source LLC
Chambersburg PA
CBHW030806230426
43667CB00008B/1086